Cohabitation and Marriage

D0262875

GREG FORSTER

Cohabitation and Marriage

A *pastoral response*

Marshall Pickering
An Imprint of HarperCollinsPublishers

Marshall Pickering is an Imprint of
HarperCollins *Religious*
Part of HarperCollins *Publishers*
77-85 Fulham Palace Road, London W6 8JB

First published in Great Britain
in 1994 by Marshall Pickering

1 3 5 7 9 10 8 6 4 2

Copyright © 1994 Greg Forster

Greg Forster asserts the moral right to be
identified as the author of this work

A catalogue record for this book is
available from the British Library

ISBN 0 551 02844-0

Typeset by Harper Phototypesetters Limited,
Northampton, England

Printed and bound in Great Britain by
HarperCollinsManufacturing Glasgow

CONDITIONS OF SALE

This book is sold subject to the condition that it shall
not, by way of trade or otherwise, be lent, re-sold, hired
out or otherwise circulated without the publisher's prior
consent in any form of binding or cover other than that
in which it is published and without a similar condition
including this condition being imposed on the
subsequent purchasers.

All rights reserved. No part of this publication may be
reproduced, stored in a retrieval system, or transmitted
in any form or by any means, electronic, mechanical,
photocopying, recording or otherwise, without the prior
permission of the publishers.

CONTENTS

A colleague of mine, rector of a nearby parish, was recently called to a hospital bedside. A man was facing a major operation, and his surgeon recommended that he marry his 'common law' wife of many years standing there and then, to make sure that she was provided for should he fail to come through the operation. For legal reasons my colleague could not help. English law does not recognize 'common law' marriage, and is quite strict about how, when and where you can marry. I do not know what the outcome of that incident was for the couple concerned. Perhaps a lawyer could have helped draw up an appropriate will, or a registrar arranged a marriage by Registrar General's licence.

This book is about that kind of situation and others like it. Not every cohabiting couple faces such dramatic circumstances, but neither are they likely to meet a surgeon who is so aware of the social problems resulting from the death of a cohabitant partner. In Britain today cohabitation outside marriage is becoming more and more common. We may approve or disapprove of that fact, or hold an open mind, reacting differently to different couples and their reasoning and behaviour. Fact it is, however, and so more and more couples are finding out the hard way what legal and social pitfalls await them if their relationship ends, whether by separation or death. That is not to mention the emotional reaction which will also be involved.

Christians have traditionally held a high view of marriage as something which at its best is an image of God's love for his people. We have also taken a poor view of sexual promiscuity and licence, in which a gift of God becomes a means of self-indulgence or power-play. I do not intend in what I write to undermine either of these views. Indeed, part of what follows will be a restatement of the Christian ideal of marriage. I do believe, however, that we need to take account of what is happening with people in a less than ideal world, and look for ways of working towards God's ideals. These are, after all, set out for the protection and well-being of all, not just as measures of how far we fail.

There is of course the danger that in writing about cohabitation in terms that are at times sympathetic I will appear to be encouraging the practice as in some way preferable to marriage. That is not my intention. There may be times when a cohabiting couple approach the Christian ideal of marriage in their relationship. There are certainly times when legally married couples fall far short of that ideal. About one tenth of divorces now take place within two years of the marriage. I want to encourage people towards that ideal from wherever they start, rather than criticizing them for having gone to the wrong starting point! Christian marriage can be seen as the destination to which we who are married travel, as much as the train which we board from the start.

But marriage is more than a sexual, moral and emotional relationship. It has certain legal benefits and offers a couple certain legal protection. I shall argue that cohabitants and their children should not be denied that protection simply because of their ignorance of the way the law is worded. The point is sometimes made that cohabitants have deliberately set out to avoid the responsibilities that go along with the benefits of marriage. That is perhaps at times the case, and I shall discuss the appropriate reaction to this view in due course, while examining the often complex reasons for cohabitation.

Tradition is what we grew up with, and for Christians it is easy to assume that the tradition which we grew up with is *the* Christian tradition, and is the correct interpretation of the Bible as well. That may be so, but we should beware of assuming it and in consequence reading back our 'traditional' attitudes and practice into the Bible. It would be fairer to say that our recent tradition has been the result of a dialogue between social conventions and expectations, contemporary pressures, and biblical interpretation.

This book has grown out of a dialogue within my own thoughts, prompted by the contemporary pressures of requests to marry cohabitant couples or baptize their children; it is shaped by the criticisms or at least the questioning looks that have aroused some strong feelings within my parish, and among fellow clergy who have been more conscious of the recent tradition (i.e. 19th & 20th century) than I; and through a desire to work within the parameters that the Bible allows, letting it criticize both that tradition and contemporary pressures. In following through those thoughts I will combine some Christian idealism about marriage and its purposes with a more functional, sociological approach to marriage and the institutions which mimic it.

Before going further I should give a preliminary definition of what I mean by cohabitation, and by marriage. More elaborate definitions and descriptions will follow.

Though the word cohabitation can be used as a polite way of describing the act of sexual intercourse, and no more, that is *not* how I intend to use it here. Nor do I mean it as a synonym for promiscuity. Some individuals' serial cohabitations are so brief that they amount to promiscuity in slow motion. Nor is the practical definition used by the DSS of so many nights together as if husband and wife within a week appropriate to my purpose. They are concerned with whether benefit is payable within the week in question. I am looking at relationships, between a man and a woman, which extend over a reasonable length of time, and in which there is a degree of permanence and commitment. How long, and how much commitment will be discussed in detail later. As we shall see, different sociologists and the lawyers in different jurisdictions have opted for various lengths of time together as their basis for study or legislation – from three months to four years. I incline towards the longer period.

The English legal definition of marriage as the lifelong partnership of one man and one woman was expressed in a court case in 1866. That reflects the Christian understanding of marriage also, and is read in a Register Office ceremony. Its intention is permanent; the commitment is freely entered into and publicly attested; it is a matter of companionship and teamwork as well as of heterosexual union. Such a partnership is entered into through a number of legally defined ceremonies. I shall discuss later whether we are right to limit the label 'marriage' only to partnerships which have those particular legally defined beginnings, or whether the law should follow custom, and recognize other beginnings. I also note that despite its definition of marriage as lifelong, English legal practice recognizes some very short-term relationships as marriage, and accepts and regulates their termination through divorce. That does not reflect the Christian ideal.

Indeed, a cynic might define marriage as that form of heterosexual relationship for whose dissolution by death or separation the state makes provision by means of divorce or inheritance laws; cohabitation is that form of relationship for which such provision is lacking. I shall suggest that that lack be remedied.

I shall use the term institution. By this I mean a pattern of ordering relationships which is shaped or defined by society at large, through its laws or customs, and not simply by the people – in this case the couple – concerned. In marriage – and I shall suggest in cohabitation also – the couple opt into a social fact, something that is already there. They do not invent it for themselves. Certainly in marrying they are also opting into a creation ordinance, for marriage was, by Christian understanding, instituted by God in the time of man's innocency. I shall consider in what follows whether those who are involved in a stable cohabitancy have opted into that same institution.

Finally, some of what I write will be applicable to other kinds of partnership, notably perhaps the partnership of a homosexual couple, or of relatives moving in together. It is not my intention that gay couples should find justification for their relationships in what I say about heterosexual cohabitants. The key moral issues involved are different in this case. Some of the legal complications, however, are the same for any unmarried individuals living together, and they, like cohabitants, would be well advised to consult lawyers.

ONE

The Way We Are

The church of which I am rector has a 'working' graveyard. We therefore see a fair number of people visiting recent graves, and leaving flowers and other tokens of grief and affection for dead relatives. Two graves in particular have caught the attention this past year for the number of flowers and other tributes placed on them since the funerals early in the year. The reasons for this are probably complex. Both were unexpected deaths, of fit men, which perhaps exacerbates the shock and the need to express grief. In both cases they had been cohabiting with the women who are now placing the floral tributes. In both cases the relationship had, as far as I can tell, been stormy, or at least interrupted, though had lasted a number of years. But the affection and the grief remains, for all that. Perhaps in the tributes there is a sense of sadness for what might have been, for things unsaid and disagreements unresolved; perhaps there is a sense of guilt – had the relationship been handled differently might the man have lived longer? – perhaps they reflect the power a particular individual could have over his friends. The grief which follows any bereavement is complex, but what I mean to show by citing these examples is that the relationship created by cohabitation is not a passing phase or casual incident in people's lives. It creates bonds of affection and feeling in just the same way as a marriage, even though it may also complicate those feelings. In both cases the 'common law wife' was left to sort out the funeral arrangements, despite uncertainty as to who was responsible, who would pay, what the blood relations would say and what the DSS (in one case) would do.

It may be argued that proper marriage would have resolved some of the problems for those couples and so left the women less grief-stricken in their loss. I do not know. It would have helped with the legal questions but I suspect that the relationships would have been just as complex and difficult – and rich – with the difficulty rooted in the character and history of the individuals involved as much as the legal framework within which they were living. Though such relationships may be listed and classified in statistics, or analysed ethically in the pages which follow, the figures and the analysis are about people with human feelings and problems. That may seem an obvious thing to say, but it is a necessary thing as well.

People and statistics

I have been writing and speaking about cohabitation for some five years now, and have been made aware of some sad cases, as well as noting some rich ones. A colleague spoke of taking the funeral of a man whose first wife had died, and who had been living with a second woman without marriage for some considerable time. The house was his, and since he died intestate his sons by his original wife inherited it. Within a week of his death they had set about evicting the woman from what was now their property. Since this was in England such action was possible. Any resistance to the eviction would have had to have been undertaken through housing legislation, or a long drawn out process of providing dependency. Had they lived in Scotland, provided they had not made public their lack of formal marriage, a far more straightforward procedure would have been available, though the courts would have still been involved. I quote this story to indicate that the statistics are not just records of what some might call a casual attitude to sexual relationships. Behind the figures lie matters of justice. Christians who denounce cohabitation on the ground that 'righteousness exalts a nation'[1] need to recognize that righteousness is a far wider concept in the Bible than merely strict sexual morality. It concerns fair treatment for the disadvantaged and powerless in society, and the shaping of law as well as attitudes so as to protect them. It does not help a homeless woman to say to her, 'You ought to have known better.'

Before going into detail about the statistics of cohabitation it is worth considering what statistics can in fact show. While Winston Churchill's saying about lies, damned lies and statistics perhaps exaggerates for effect, it does remind us that statistics can be 'used,' and that without analysis and interpretation they can be misleading. It may appear damning that those who cohabit before marriage are 60 per cent more likely to split within 10 years of marriage, but John Haskey of the Office of Population Censuses and Surveys, whose article[2] explores this statistic is very clear in stating that no *causal* connection is demonstrated merely by the figures. And in connection with the stability of cohabitation, it may be revealing that a study in America (admittedly over ten years ago) did not find enough couples who had cohabited for ten years to make a statistically valid sample. Most had split – some had married.[3] But as Haskey reminded us, it is to underlying attitudes that we need to look for explanations of this rather than at the mere absence of a marriage certificate. The statistics pose questions, rather than giving answers.

It may be true that half of those currently marrying have lived together, or at least given the same address, before marriage. That is a statistic. What it does not tell us is the length of time they have lived together, or their reasons. It may not even tell us whether they have been 'cohabiting' in the sense that I have used it here, or in a way in which sociologists or the DSS might define it. For instance, I recently took the wedding of a couple who gave the same address when they arranged the service; they were due to take possession of the house the next week, I think. In practice over the months before the wedding a hoped-for job transfer did not take place, and whatever their intentions had been the girl was at her parents' address more often than at the home she jointly owned with her fiancé elsewhere. Statistics do not tell the whole truth. Again, in former generations even if not currently, one parental address may appear on the marriage registers, with the groom (say) genuinely *lodging* there, perhaps as an apprentice away from home, prior to the wedding, rather than paying rent elsewhere.

That being said, statistics will indicate trends and expose the extent of a situation, without revealing the details, or the reasons that lie behind the trend. They should in no way, however, be regarded as deterministic. It may be a good conversational gambit for a clergyman talking to a cohabitant couple about their forthcoming marriage, to tell them that the statistics are against them. Not only is such a comment a bit late for the couple concerned (though non-cohabitants might do well to weigh that before moving in together); it is also not correct. What is against the permanence of the relationship is the couple's own attitudes, not the figures, which are simply recording the effects of others' attitudes on their lives.

Cohabitation and divorce

Erstwhile cohabitants are apparently twice as likely to have split as married couples. In evaluating that statistic we need to ask what definition of 'cohabitation' was used by the person conducting the survey. A definition of a mere three months together will skew the statistic towards impermanence and insecurity, while a definition of at least three years together, for the sake of argument, will produce a very different result. Within those figures there will be those who hoped for permanence, but were denied it, and also those who never regarded their relationship as other than casual, and part of a possible series.

Even those who regard their relationship as casual will have an emotional and personal investment in it, I believe, which will affect them probably more than they realize. There will also have been some financial implications, if only that they had not retained accommodation in their own name. Even though I would not want to think of such casual relationships even as quasi-marriage, I believe that the statistics do demonstrate the extent of this as a problem. A problem it is, and even individuals caught up in the splitting of these relationships ought to have the benefit of a 'divorce law substitute' to regulate the division of property. Such casual relationships will skew the statistics and shed a bad light on those who cohabit with more permanent intent.

It is not the statistics which determine whether a previously cohabitant married couple will divorce, but their understanding of marriage and their attitude to commitment. This may have been latent in their readiness to cohabit in the first place. (Or, conversely, those with a strong view of married commitment may be less likely to start their life together without the formal tie.) The statistics serve a useful purpose in highlighting the tendency; its explanation and remedy lie elsewhere, and it is not inevitable that a couple's future will be determined by the trend. It is even possible that the figures are skewed retrospectively; someone whose marriage has broken down may more readily tell a researcher about its uncertain beginnings, out of bitterness or remorse.

A further danger in casual use of statistics is the way publicists and moralists present them in a negative way. So 30 per cent of marriages end in divorce, and this is part of a rising trend. That is not good, if you believe that stable marriage is important for the individual, for the couple together and their children, and for society at large. But if 30 per cent are divorcing, that actually means that 70 per cent are sticking together for better or worse, despite the pressures and examples around them and the greater ease of obtaining a divorce. The cup is more than half full, not almost half empty.

Strictly, also, the often quoted media figure that one marriage in three ends in divorce is not correct. We do not yet know how many of this year's marriages will end in divorce. We can relate the number of divorces to the number of marriages within the year, and that is currently running at a ratio of about 1:2.2. The fact that the ratio is rising is only partly due to the rise in divorces, which have run at about 163,000 a year for almost ten years, during which time the number of marriages has fallen by about one tenth to 365,000 in 1990. Haskey has some figures on this. In his survey sample the cumulative percentage of women who had divorced by the fifteenth anniversary of their (first) wedding was likely to be over 10 per cent among those who had not cohabited before marriage, and about 15 per cent among those who had. If the number who had separated is added into those figures, they come out as 14 per cent and 22 per cent respectively. He points out that if the length of the union, both before and after the actual marriage ceremony, is taken into account then the differential is less, but is still there; the respective figure after fifteen years *together* would be over 10 per cent and just over 12 per cent.[4]

One thing this statistic does appear to show is that the idea of cohabitation as a trial for marriage is not valid, at least among those who come to marriage. But even that is not completely true. It may have proved a valid trial for those who decided their relationship was wrong, though some of those might have stayed together constructively if they had had the support of the institution behind them. It may also have been that the initial hesitation, which led to delay in ratifying the relationship, reflected a weakness that was there in the relationship irrespective of how it developed and which in turn led to the breakdown.

How prevalent is cohabitation?

Since cohabitation is by definition a relationship that is not marked by any registered beginning, or end, precise figures are hard to come by. General Booth, commenting on parts of London at the turn of the century, recognizes the fact of couples living together without marriage.[5] My own parish registers in what was then a Cheshire village skirting the Manchester commuter belt, record eight marriages between 1900 and 1915 in which the couple were resident at the same address. They are recorded more precisely than normal, as if my predecessor was indicating his disapproval of what he had to record. But that is a record of the relationships which came to the altar. Others did not, such as one during the 1920s of which I was told a few years ago. Though the couple lived together and had children, there is no record of the cohabitation even in the registers of the children's baptism, for my predecessor at that time refused to record the father's name, though he was present at the baptisms openly acknowledging his children. Quite understandably his daughter, who told me of this, was not happy with how it had been handled. Apparently he had a legal wife still living, so that marriage was, for that working-class couple, out of the question.

Even more recently the practice is less than well recorded. Karen Dunnell's study in 1976 was the first major survey in this country to ask questions about couples' relationships before marriage, and to reveal the extent of cohabitation. It was based on a sample of 6,589 women aged between sixteen and fifty.[6] (They felt that to question couples would complicate the survey, and perhaps lead to conflicting answers!) Her report reads as if it came as a surprise to the survey team to discover that 2 per cent of those who appeared to be married were not in fact legally bound; their questions had not been specifically designed to reveal this, and so the actual percentage may have been rather greater than this. Of those 'married' only once, 1 per cent were in fact cohabitant; of those in the sample who had been divorced the percentage was 30 percent. The proportion whose first marriage began with cohabitation rose from 1 per cent of those married between 1956-60 to 9 per cent of those married between 1971-5, The older the women in the sample were at the time of their first marriage, the more likely it was to have begun as cohabitation. The more recent the marriage at the time of the survey, the longer this period of cohabitation was likely to have been, though the sample was too small by this time to give any reliable trend.

Dunnell's apparent surprise at the occurrence of cohabitation is perhaps only to be expected. Even in the 1973 edition of Professor R. Fletcher's study of *The Family and Marriage in*

Britain[7] cohabitation does not get a mention, though premarital intercourse (then, according to Dunnell's findings, running at around 50 percent between future spouses) does. He waxes lyrical about the continuing reduction in the age at marriage, and the bright prospects for marriage and the family as the source of companionship and stability in society for the future, despite the dire and statistically inaccurate forebodings of certain clerics. He even sees in a rise in the divorce rate a sign of higher expectations for a style of marriage based on equality of respect and companionship, as much as falling standards. Perhaps he was right, but the significance of his book for our purposes is that even this professor of sociology missed the coming development of so significant a feature of family life. It was not yet on the social agenda, though by the time Fletcher wrote maybe 3 per cent of marriages were beginning that way.

Dunnell's survey showed perhaps 2 per cent of women between sixteen and fifty cohabiting. Since her work in 1976 the figure has risen dramatically, so that in the year 1988/9 the figure (for eighteen to fifty year old women) was 7.7 per cent and in the eighteen and twenty-four age range it was 12.4 per cent. The peak age for men to cohabit is slightly older than women, 13 per cent of those between twenty-five and twenty-nine doing so. This perhaps reflects the tendency for men to marry older, and to pick slightly younger partners. The figures from the Government's publication *Social Trends 21* (1991) also show that the number of women who cohabited with their husband-to-be rose to 53 per cent in 1987. It is currently higher still. This is not quite comparable with Dunnell's figures because it includes second and subsequent marriages – about a third of the total. Of these a far higher proportion than first marriages begin with cohabitation, as Dunnell did note.

The length of cohabitation prior to marriage is not noted in *Social Trends 21*, but it appears to be growing, as Dunnell suspected. In her sample more than half had been together less than a year at the time of marriage. In a far less scientific sample based on the 150 couples marrying in this church in South Manchester in the last eight years, 20 per cent had lived together before marriage, and two thirds of those had been together for over a year.

I suggested that Professor Fletcher had missed a trend that was developing before his eyes. If that was true of him in the 1960s, then it has been even more true of the church in the seventies and eighties. My colleague Gary Jenkins surveyed a number of North London parishes[8] – mostly evangelical – in 1988 and found a wide range of responses to the problem. Two thirds of those who responded did not make any special arrangements for the preparation of those who were cohabiting; one in eight claimed not to know how many of those who came to them were cohabiting. On the other hand, one third regarded the relationship as sinful while about a quarter regarded the relationship as right to some degree, even if not ideal. In a straw poll that I conducted in 1991 at a conference of clergy aged over forty, also evangelicals, a similar spread of views was found among those who selected themselves to discuss the subject; some regarding the act of intercourse as consummating the marriage even before it had been pledged; others (just under half my sample) regarding it as inherently sinful; few making any distinction in their preparation except to place less emphasis on the physical and sexual side of marriage. If Dunnell found as long ago as 1976 that 74 per cent of couples had made love before their marriage even that distinction was possibly outdated. In both my survey and Jenkins' a minority of respondents commented on the social dimension of marriage (two sevenths of Jenkins' sample), and none on its significance for the wider family – though perhaps those who referred to society did include the partners' families. I suspect that for most of us the issue had crept up, unsuspected, and we had found ourselves conducting the marriages of cohabitants without giving or having the time for preparation of any special teaching for such couples. A number of my respondents indicated that they were rethinking the matter. Some ideas for such a rethink are included as an appendix.

But what of those who do not appear in the marriage statistics? How else may we gauge the proportion of those cohabiting, and their attitudes to their relationship? In 1989 the proportion of births outside marriage rose to 26.6 per cent. By 1991 it was about 30 per cent (Source: *Social Trends 23*), with 22 per cent of the overall total registered jointly by father and mother, and 13 per cent of the total – one in eight – registered with both unmarried parents at the same address. This represents a rise from about 9 per cent in 1976, of whom only half were jointly registered. This can be interpreted in either a pessimistic or an optimistic way. It does seem to indicate more willingness to accept responsibilities by unmarried fathers (even if that willingness may be unrecognized by the law). On the other hand it indicates a greater reluctance to accept a commitment to the mother as wife – or perhaps an unwillingness to accept the relevance of such a formal commitment in their relationship. The proportion of marriages between conception and birth declined by 19 per cent between 1976 and 1988, during which time the proportion of joint registrations of births outside marriage rose by 360 per cent. The sad side of the figures is that in that period the proportion of pregnancies outside marriage that were terminated also rose – by 160 per cent.

These figures represent both an improvement and decline in standards. That is reflected in the more personal impression which I get from this parish. Of the hundred or so applications for baptism that I have received in the past three years, perhaps twenty have been for the baptism of children of unmarried mothers. In a few other cases the circumstances were so chaotic that we got no further than an enquiry by the baby's grandmother about a christening, so I do not know whether the parents were cohabiting or not. In ten of these instances the mother appeared to be on her own, either from the start, or by the time the request for baptism was made maybe a year or more after birth. The remaining ten came from cohabitant couples, some of whom referred to their intention to marry in due course, while others regarded their existing arrangement as acceptable morally and for their practical purposes. Only one of these couples has so far approached me about the wedding, but that was deferred several times for financial reasons; the man received an unexpectedly large tax bill in connection with his self-employed contract work, and hopes of paying for the wedding evaporated. Nevertheless, they were there together at the local school nativity play last Christmas, proudly watching their son taking part. In another case it is the father who is actively and responsibly involved in arranging his son's schooling. Of the other eighty baptisms recorded over that period I know of at least three families where a wedding has taken place since the first child was born and baptised some years ago, and another where a properly married couple have split after a blazing, public row.

Those details are strictly anecdotal. In statistical terms it is a very small sample and is self-selecting in that some parents in those circumstances do not want anything to do with religion, or feel they can't ask anyway. It also depends very much on how much I have been able to keep up with a particular couple. Nevertheless, it shows the sort of situations that come up in what is a fairly normal, socially mixed parish. I draw no firm conclusions from this picture, except the platitude that life is not neat and tidy, and rarely matches our ideal image.

Notes

1. E.g. the peroration on p.24 of Ted Pratt's booklet, *Living in Sin,* Portsmouth 1991.
2. John Haskey, 'Pre-Marital Cohabitation and the Probability of Subsequent Divorce': analysis using new data from the General Household Survey, in *Population Trends 68 Summer 1992.* Office of Population Censuses and Surveys. Haskey analyses his sample in age-groups, and actually says 'the differentials (between divorcees who had cohabited prior to marriage and those who had not) are quite large – sometimes there is a factor of two between corresponding proportions.' While in all age groups the proportion

of those who split was greater among those who had previously cohabited, in some groups the difference was only 1 per cent.

3. P. Blumstein & P. Schwartz, *American Couples, Money, Work, Sex,* NY 1983, quoted in Tim Stafford, *Sexual Chaos,* IVP Leicester 1993 (Illinois 1989) p.116. According to Stafford's summary, they too note that cohabitants are 'between two and four times as likely' to split as married couples, though he fails to quote the actual rates.

4. Haskey, *op.cit.,* p.16f. These percentages are quoted approximately since they are derived from a graph. They are also based on standardised projections rather than an actual sample.

5. Cited in Joan Perkin, *Women and Marriage in 19th Century England*, Routledge, London 1989 p.158.

6. Karen Dunnell, *Family Formation* 1976, HMSO London. 1979.

7. Pelican, Harmondsworth, 1973 (previous editions 1962 & 1965), pp.234-265. Fletcher can be as critical of the trendy left with its denunciation of family life as of conservative moralists lamenting a supposedly lost past. He mixed an optimistic utilitarian ethic with his sociology. I am tempted to liken him to Voltaire's Dr Pangloss, seeing everything in the best possible light, but that is perhaps too easy to do in retrospect.

8. Unpublished pastoral studies dissertation at Oak Hill Theological College, written up subsequently as *Cohabitation, a biblical perspective.* Grove Books, Nottingham 1992. See p.22.

TWO

How We Got Here

Oh, a blacksmith courted me, nine months and better,
   He fairly won my heart, wrote me a letter,
With his hammer in his hand he looked so clever,
   and if I were with my love I'd live for ever.

Strange news is come to town, strange news is carried;
   strange news flies up and down, that my love's married!
Oh! I wish them both much joy, though they do not hear me,
   and may God reward them well for the slighting of me!

What did you promise me when you lay beside me
   You said you'd marry me, and not deny me.
'If I said I'd marry you it was only for to try you,
   go and bring your witness, love, and I'll not deny you.'

'Oh! witness have I none, save God almighty,
   and may he reward you well for the slighting of me, . . .'
And her lips grew pale and wan, her poor heart was a-tremble
   for to think that she'd loved one who'd proved deceitful.

                                          *Trad. Anon**

It is easy to create a picture of the past which is a projection of some ideal, or the justification of some present ideology. This is true of the history of marriage as of other features of society. Beryl Rawson begins a book on Roman family life and structure[1] with three quotations from previous classical historians; in one the Roman family is seen as a paragon; in the next the dregs of social behaviour flow down the Tiber, while the third

*An English folk song dating, by its contents, from before 1750, or at least when ideas from that period were still current.

opts for something between the two. Though they all write within ten years of each other, all, says Rawson, are oversimplified, not least because they each select their preferred evidence from the restricted field of Roman literature, and ignore material which is available from archeological sources, and such documents as legal and medical texts.

A similar point could be made with reference to studies of mediaeval and modern marriage in Britain. One author will trace the origins of 'companionate' marriage – in which the couple select each other for companionship and love – in the early middle ages; another will stress the strains this same recent form of spouse-selection imposes on twentieth century marriage.[2]

Roman marriage

Reference to Roman marriage is relevant to this study, partly because it represents the background to the New Testament even if Rome's eastern provinces (to which most of the NT was directed) may not have shown quite the same pattern as Italy, where the most accessible evidence is found. It also represents the background to the writings of Tertullian, Hippolytus and Augustine, which have shaped the development of Christian thinking about marriage down to the text of the Book of Common Prayer, if not longer.

The picture of marriage in early imperial Rome was complex, and practice did not always match the legal or ethical theories. (I, too, must be careful not to read back our present into the Roman past, but this is the conclusion of Rawson and her colleagues.) It was complicated by the stratification of society, and different marriage laws were applied to citizens, resident subjects of the Empire, freemen, freedmen, slaves, and to men and women within these categories. While there were several formal marriage ceremonies, which conferred different degrees of bond and ritual status to the parties and their offspring, 'the most common form of marriage involved no essential ceremonial and was based on enduring cohabitation.'³ In this form the wife did not come wholly under her husband's authority, but retained links with her family of birth, and kept her own property. To be valid a marriage required that the partners be eligible, and that they lived together with marital intention and regard. There were, however, traditional ceremonies of betrothal which helped to establish beforehand this marital intention, and were frequently observed. In Roman law the key elements in a marriage were intention and consent – *affectio maritalis*.

However, there were limits on who was eligible to marry, and whom they might marry. Some of Hippolytus' strictures about immoral relationships have this background. Marriage was not possible in law between slave and free, or between citizens and others. Indeed, a free person living as married with a slave might be reduced in some circumstances to slave status. Nevertheless, such unions did occur, and had recognition as *contubernia* – messing down in the same tent – despite criticism, especially if the woman was well-born. In cases where one party was slave and the other free, proper marriage might be recognised on the freeing of the slave party. Despite this prejudice and the changes and chances of slavery there is evidence that family units based on *contubernia* survived many years. No doubt many foundered, but tombstones and other monuments bear witness to those that thrived. Much of the evidence seems to come from Caesar's household⁴ which sheds particular light on the background of Paul's letters if his 'Captivity' letters are from Rome, with Philippians 4:22 referring to the same people.

The great anxiety of early imperial legislators seems to have been the lack of children, at least in the noble families. After infant mortality the average number of children in such families seems to have been no more than two, and some died out. There seems to have been acceptance of barrenness as a reason for divorce, and perhaps pressure to divorce and seek children from a second wife. Nevertheless, a husband might record on his wife's grave that though she had offered such a divorce, he had refused it because of the partnership and loyalty they enjoyed. Such general concern in Roman society for fecundity, as much as his biblical studies, may lie behind Augustine's teaching (reiterated in the BCP) that one of the chief 'goods' of marriage is the bearing of children.[5]

The undercurrents in society are notoriously difficult to gauge in historical times. One cannot use oral history to tap illiterate sources, since they are long silent. Rawson, all the same, does make some attempt She notes that our sources are almost exclusively male[6] but suggests that the male ideology of what marriage should bring was not always fulfilled; 'In Rome' (as opposed to modern society where she sees wives as the frustrated ones) 'it may have been the husbands who were disappointed when their wives declined to assume the limited, domestic role that they were told had been that of their ancestors.' (p.26) She notes that even as early as 195 BC women successfully protested against the role cast for them as wastrels in laws against excessive consumption, and as quoted above that some marriages were ones of equality and partnership. Is she, too, being anachronistic in seeing a female value-system, which could be aware of such possibilities as contraception, running beneath and against the dominant male ideology? Perhaps we have too little evidence, but such questions are relevant to the interpretation of such passages as Ephesians 5, where, as I shall suggest later, Paul was not simply repeating the conventional male-dominated morality.

The early church – against the Tide

Conventional expectations and Christian reassessment of them form the background to the arguments in the early years of the third century in Rome between the later Pope Callistus and a rival, Hippolytus. It appears that the church had recognized the unions of slave women and their masters, since the women had little choice in the matter, and had attempted to impose church discipline on the men if they were Christians, expecting both parties to be monogamous and faithful to each other, even though in terms of Roman law the union could never be a proper marriage. Callistus, himself an ex-slave, wanted the church to treat women who consorted with their male slaves in the same way, recognizing and enforcing the relationship as marriage, even though in Roman law such a union might lead to the free woman being reduced to slavery. Hippolytus was scandalized. It is difficult at this distance, with very little of their writings to go on, to see how much Christian moral sense and how much their own social milieux influenced each protagonist. The dilemmas posed by slavery remained with the church for a further ten centuries, but the verdict of tradition has gone with Callistus, even if at the time he may have been pushing a dangerous, anti-social innovation as far as pagan Rome was concerned.[7]

Prior to the Roman debate just described, and in less controversial circumstances, the Bishop of Antioch, Ignatius, wrote in about AD 107 to a younger colleague, Polycarp, urging that to avoid lust-driven unions it was 'fitting that those who marry should make their unions with the bishop's consent (or advice) so that the marriage should be according to the Lord's standards. . .[8]

Tertullian, a North African lawyer and heterodox Christian who joined the Montanist sect in later life and also flourished at the turn of the second and third centuries, went further and enthusiastically regarded a marriage as completed with the blessing of the church. However, still writing 'to his wife'[9] he seems to suggest that a marriage undertaken before conversion was sanctified, or even sacramentalized, by that conversion and the attendant baptism. His comments on the union of slaves with free women perhaps illuminate Hippolytus' strictures. There were obviously stories going the rounds about high-class pagan women who consorted with eunuch slaves for lustful pleasure without the risk of children.

The influence of Augustine is considerable in the church's views of marriage. How much his theology was influenced by his personal history is a moot point, but his views are not dis-

qualified just because he had a past. That past was firmly rooted in the ambiguities of late Roman society, with its anxieties
over raising children to preserve one's name and pray at one's
grave, and with its tolerance of many levels of commitment
from prostitution to binding marriage. Overlaid on this is
Augustine's post-conversion distress at what the church saw as
the sexual immorality of the age, and its suspicion of passion as
a motive even within marriage – passion meaning loss of rational control over one's actions and feelings. This fear of passion
stemmed as much from the philosophers of the day as from biblical teaching. Thus he can write very tenderly of his attraction
for the concubine with whom he had lived for a number of
years, and who had borne him a child, but whom he had sent
away when his mother arranged a decent marriage for him. The
marriage, in the end, seems never to have taken place. But he
also looked back on his arrangement with this unnamed
woman as something that was 'a contract of love based on lust'.
He speaks of the girl as one who was his 'comrade, but one
whom I had found by a wandering *passio* empty of wisdom'.[10]
He also writes at a later period in his life (in words which echo
classical sentiment) of true friendship only to be expected
between man and man, and hardly in marriage. Thus in his
own person he lived out the dilemmas of Christians of his age,
moving through pagan concubinage, projected marriage and
conversion to celibate episcopacy.

Brooke (p.67) highlights the contrast between this state of
affairs, which was quite acceptable socially and which would
have been true of the first century as well as the fourth, and
the high ideals of marriage portrayed in the New Testament.
His point is valid, though if we remember that the words for
husband and wife could equally be rendered man and woman
in NT Greek, it might be that St. Paul is not saying 'everyone
must adopt the highest level of legal marriage' – many of
them legally could not; his message may be that 'man and
wife/*contubernalis*/concubine must show a level of love
which reflects Christ's love for the church'; an equally

demanding, but slightly different, message.

To return to Augustine, his key contribution to the Christian ideal of marriage was to identify and encourage pursuit of the 'goods' in marriage. Writing to nuns, he speaks of the good of marriage to be found in fidelity, childbearing and the binding oath (*sacramentum* – a soldier's oath of allegiance) which made it lifelong. His purpose was to persuade them that marriage was not a lesser calling than their asceticism, but at times he struggled against his own arguments. He regarded even intercourse within marriage as unavoidably tainted with lust.[11] It is from these goods, somewhat altered, that the 'causes for which marriage was ordained' in the Prayer Book are derived. He seems to have regarded childrearing as the prime good in marriage, but he is ambivalent; he speaks of his own love-child, apparently, when he says '. . .when a child is born against its parents' wish.'

Into the Middle Ages – the sublime and the ridiculous

While nuptial blessings are found within the church's services as early as Tertullian, and hints as to how these were expressed in liturgical action are found in Gregory of Nazianzus (Asia Minor, c.AD390) and Ambrose (Milan, fl.AD370) no full marriage service is described until a letter of Pope Nicholas, dated AD866, which speaks of espousal, the giving of a ring and gifts before witnesses, and a Mass followed by a blessing as the couple leave.[12] Despite this, marriage was a civil institution, which did not have to be conducted before the church, but which the church might seek to hallow. It was not a Christian institution which impinged on the wider society. Nevertheless the church did attempt during the post Roman era to impose Christian morals, as it understood them, on society. Thus the law code of Wihtred (King of Kent in the early 8th century) imposes penalties on adultery – though no doubt pagan husbands had not looked gladly on it – and on intercourse outside marriage.

The church also sought to prevent incest, so that by the 6th century marriage between second cousins was forbidden and cousinage was defined not simply as a blood tie, or one of affinity through marriage, but also as something conferred by 'gossipry' – i.e. through godparents and godchildren. Such strictures could get out of hand. Mediaeval jurists discussed (apparently seriously) whether a father had acquired a forbidden degree of relationship to his wife by unintentionally accepting his own child back from the priest at the font – a role restricted to godfathers. By the 11th century the forbidden degrees of cousinage had extended to the sixth degree – though after a few decades of dispensations and pardons these rules were rescinded as impractical. (At the Reformation, England at least reverted to the simple list of forbidden degrees found in Leviticus.) Such an obsession with the dangers of sexual sins of this obscure kind may seem laughable to us, but they explain one reason why the church became more involved in the legalities of marriage; only the clergy were able to protect society from these sins through their knowledge of canon law. Over this period, too, there was an increasing rigour in clerical and monastic discipline, and a heightened regard for the sacramental nature of marriage and other rites of the church – *sacramentum* now having taken on its full theological meaning. Both these features of church life will have had their spin-off in attitudes to informal marriage. The place of affection in marriage was also being legally recognized, as that meaning of the phrase *affectio maritalis* was deliberately allowed to slip into the discussion.

Concubinage was still regarded as a legitimate form of relationship, and so too was marriage without the presence of a priest or a nuptial blessing. It seems that part of the poignance of the story of Abélard and Héloise is that they did marry in church in the presence of a priest, but were forced to go back on it. That story too shows up something of the double standards within the church, which from the late Roman period had been preaching against marriage for clergy, but tolerated concubinage even in cathedral closes. (Some at the time would defend this in the grounds that if Paul had said that a bishop should have only one wife, he could have a wife.) Even as late as the English Pope, Adrian IV, it was a real question to ask whether slaves might marry, even with their owner's consent. (He answered yes, on the grounds that in Christ there is neither bond nor free.) Now double standards, and the legacy of slavery and secular custom, do not prove that the church was wrong to insist on formal marriages in church. At the same time there was a growing insistence in the eleventh and twelfth centuries on legitimacy as a prerequisite for inheritance among the landed classes. That does not prove that economics ruled pastoral theology.[13] It does demonstrate that the church wrestled with complex personal and social problems, some of its own making, in upholding standards of sexual morality. Perhaps it does show that the range of options between very clear, church-blessed marriage and the unmarried but cohabiting state was not as clear cut for at least half of Christian history as it had become in England by the time of the 1949 Marriage Act.

The process by which marriage as an institution in England has got to a state in which it now is is not entirely clear. In particular, the 'betrothed' state seems to have been ambiguous during the middle ages. While by the late middle ages the church regarded the public marriage ceremony (in the church porch – see Brooke, ch.10) as the main event and in 1439 finally defined it as a sacrament, officially, for many of the lay people it was the contractual arrangements which preceded it which legitimated the relationship. These would be made privately but known publicly. After these, intercourse and a common roof were widely expected. Some clergy, however, seem to have accepted this pattern of events, while many lay people seem to have followed the church's ideal of delaying the move to shared accommodation until after the nuptial ceremony. Church courts saw nuptials as marriage and the canons of 1604 insisted that they take place between 8am and noon in the parish church of one of the couple after banns, but popular morality focused on the earlier espousals. Archdeacons' courts until the time of the Stuarts had power to bring action against couples who had intercourse outside marriage, including those who were betrothed.[14] They seem rarely to have done so in the case of the betrothed.

Modern Marriage Law in England –
a Secular Institution?

The English Marriage Act of 1753 brought forward by Lord Chancellor Hardwicke marks a turning point. It had a history, and that background is not very creditable. Despite the 1604 canons there were clergy who would solemnize a marriage (for a price) at the drop of a hat, and those in certain allegedly extra-diocesan chapels (especially near the Fleet Prison in London) blatantly disregarded the canons, and against them there was no 'ordinary' who could act. Since the latter half of the seventeenth century there had been a tax on marriages which encouraged attempts at tax evasion with the connivance of the 'Fleet Parsons,' by those who did want a formal marriage.

There were still those who were content to use customary marriage, without priest or church, making promises and (if they owned the property to make it relevant) agreeing to marriage contracts and settlements and then consummating the relationship. Since a Fleet Marriage was legally binding even if it had been conducted in an uncanonical manner without observing the obligation to give public notice or wait while it was published, rich heiresses were (their families feared) prey to the attentions of any gigolo who might catch their eye and win their hand and fortune. Such were the fears expressed (in more parliamentary language) by the landed gentry and peers who voted in Lord Hardwicke's Act. Some, to be fair, argued that the cost of banns or a licence might deter the less well-to-do from marrying; others wished that public opinion would allow their legislation to apply only to the landed classes – but they recognized that England in the 1750s was too liberal to allow one law for the rich and another for the poor. It seems that a vast proportion of the poorer classes of London resorted to the Fleet for their weddings, partly by custom and partly for the greater privacy of a clandestine wedding.

Some of the Parliamentarians also prided themselves in their enlightenment thinking on dispensing with the sacramental idea of marriage, for the law insisted that unless the legal requirements were met, of banns being read or a licence obtained, and a public ceremony being conducted by a properly authorised clerk in holy orders between people who were of age, or if under twenty-one had their parents' consent, even a fully sacramental ceremony was void, and the parson who knowingly conducted it might face fourteen years' transportation. Thus did the gentry protect their inheritances, and the Government its tax revenue of five shillings per marriage certificate.[15] When in 1755 a similar bill was proposed for Scotland it failed because the Kirk held that it infringed their religion as enshrined in the Act of Union. English custom was, of course, not secularized as easily as the law, and in the nineteenth and twentieth centuries a church wedding became a sign of respectability and a means of acknowledging a deep meaning in life and love, rather than an unwelcome public appearance.[16]

It is easy to smile (from our safe distance) at the eighteenth century. The growth of cities and social mobility and (as Stone argues) the growth of liberal ideas about individual autonomy was making informal marriage among the poorer classes less stable. It was more easily broken by a simple move from home.[17] Among the landed classes there was certainly the fear of the heir or heiress falling prey to some inappropriate match, sealed irrevocably by a clandestine marriage, though whether the reality justified the fear it is difficult to gauge at this distance. Far more ordinary people used clandestine marriage than ever the gentry did. Was it like some social ills today, where the odd case inflated by rumour begets a thousand neuroses by the time it reaches Parliament?

Lord Hardwicke's Act did remedy many abuses, and clarify

the law of marriage in England. Its target was clandestine marriage, but by insisting on marriage in the Parish Church (though allowing concessions to Jews and Quakers) it invalidated any of the previous 'common law' customary marriage practices, and drove conscientious non-conformists into bastardy for several generations. In England 'Common Law Marriage' ceased to exist in law, though it has persisted in common parlance, and I have spoken in the 1990s with people who still believe it to have some legal force. It is a long time a-dying! This is perhaps because it still exists in Scots law – though the dramatic elopements to Gretna Green, or Coldstream and a number of other places just over the border were not for 'Common Law' Marriages which depend on shared residence but for the then still far laxer Scots legal wedding. Not until 1940 was Scots law tightened up to require 21 days residence before marriage.[18]

By insisting on a legal framework and no other for valid marriage (even though that framework was until 1837 the Established Church) Lord Hardwicke's Act reversed the church's claim and triumph of the 12th to 15th centuries, that marriage was an ecclesiastical matter not a civil one, a sacrament (in which the couple by their promises and actions were its priests) as much as a contract. I suggest that this is a different step from that made among the Romans in 1563 (the council of Trent) when they required the presence of a priest for the validity of a marriage. That affirmed the church's place in marriage as a sacrament. In theory at least it is only marriages before a priest that Roman Catholics consider valid. In contrast, Lord Hardwicke's supporters affirmed the secular, enlightened, state as the arbiter of marriage.[19] This was merely extended by subsequent Marriage Acts, especially the one of 1836, which made for more rigid registration, and established registrars as a secular alternative to the Anglican clergy as officiants. In so doing provision was also made for conscientious non-conformists. The resulting Anglican position is to recognize both secular and ecclesiastical marriages as equally valid and binding.

Property and divorce

At the time of Lord Hardwicke's Act the only form of divorce available was by a special Act of Parliament – available only to the rich and influential – though the working class folk custom of selling at a public market an unwanted wife (no doubt on many occasions by arrangement to her lover) persisted into the next century. Various divorce laws were passed in the later nineteenth and twentieth centuries, culminating in the present Acts of 1969 and 1984, which claim to focus on the breakdown of marriage, but actually list five corroborating facts to substantiate the breakdown which the man or woman may cite as grounds for divorce; adultery, desertion, unreasonable behaviour, five year separation, or two years' separation and mutual consent. A petition may be filed after one year of marriage. Thus the commitment implied legally in a marriage ceremony is considerably different in 1994 from that in 1754.

Another relevant change is the Married Women's Property Act of 1882, which removed the main argument that had lain behind Hardwicke's Act. Women could now retain their own property after marriage; no longer might the penniless gigolo walk off with an heiress' fortune. This and subsequent legislation has made marriage more a partnership between legal equals. It is perhaps worth noting that in the early years of the nineteenth century up to one fifth of the population still may have been cohabiting. Apart from the conscientious objectors to the use of the Established Church, there were women who knew when they would be better off financially. In marrying, a woman would lose control of her property and income, such as it might be. But before 1834 (when the Poor Law was emended) she might obtain a maintenance order against her child's father, giving her an independent income from him. Some preferred this to marriage.[20] Even today, despite the changes in women's rights, one motive for cohabitation seems to be the woman's desire to maintain greater financial independence.[21]

It remains to ask whether any of these historical circumstances bears upon the present phenomena of cohabitation. I say 'phenomena' because there are several patterns of cohabitation, not just one. Where some kind of formal contract is agreed upon we can see a direct parallel with the mediaeval espousal contracts, which people treated as a binding marriage even if they did not lead to the church door. The difference is that mediaeval espousal contracts usually involved the fathers as well as the parties to the marriage themselves. We still have to ask what kinds of contract might in our circumstances be treated as marital. For much of the period discussed church expectations and popular opinions were at variance, and the church was able to live and work with popular views, even if it upheld something fuller. Perhaps this 'more robust attitude'[22] towards cohabitation – the ability to teach the value and possibility of the ideal, while living with the imperfect – has something to commend it, though it belonged in an age that was less mobile and less bureaucratic.

Notes

1. *The Family in Ancient Rome,* ed. B. Rawson, Croom Helm, London & Sydney, 1986, p.1.
2. Contrast the lines taken by A. McFarlane, *Marriage and Love in England, 1300-1840* Oxford, 1986 & J. Dominian in *Marriage Faith and Love* (p.86) & L. Stone *Family, Sex and Marriage in England, 1500-1840* OUP, NY.
3. *op. cit.* p.15f.
4. P.R.C. Weaver, in Rawson *op. cit.* p.145ff. The link with Paul's letters is mine (Rawson's book explicitly avoids the Christian evidence as being mostly too late to be relevant to their period). Even if, as I think the case, the captivity letters come from Caesarea, the people of Caesar's establishment there would be drawn from this same group, so Paul was living and writing with such people and their relationships in mind.
5. e.g. *De Nuptiis et Concupiscentia,* I.iv ff. & *passim.*
6. The first example of a letter written by a Roman woman was not published until after Rawson's book. It comes from Hadrian's wall.

7. *The Treaties on the Apostolic Constitutions of St Hippolytus of Rome*, ed. G. Dix & H. Chadwick, SPCK London, 1968. See the Introduction, p.xvii, and the text. xvi,6,7,23,24, together with the editors' notes *in loco*.

8. *Ad Polycarpum* ch. 5. Is he advocating the bishop as marriage broker?

9. *Ad Uxorem. II.8* in *Ancient Christian Writers XIII, Treatises on Marriage and Remarriage* ed. Wm. T. P. Le Saint, S. J., Longmans Green, London 1951 *Ad Uxorem* probably belongs to his orthodox period c.AD200.

10. *Confessions*, IV.2;2f.

11. When the present pope, shortly after his consecration, spoke about the sin of lust within marriage someone accused him of inventing a new sin. They were wrong, by some 1,600 years.

12. cf. C. H. Hutchins, *Liturgy for Marriage,* Grove, Nottingham 1976, and in *Anglican Worship Today*, Collins, London 1980 p.185.

13. In this section I have referred extensively to Christopher Brooke, *The Mediaeval Idea of Marriage*, OUP Oxford 1989, *passim*.

14. So Alan McFarlane, *Marriage and Love in England, 1300-1840*, Blackwell, Oxford & NY 1986 p.305. His main thesis in the book is to argue for the distinctiveness of the English pattern of courtship by the couple themselves and marriage for companionship.

15. The story is told in L. Stone, *The Family, Sex and Marriage in England*, Harmondsworth, 1979 (2nd edition) pp. 28-36, and in R. L. Brown's paper in *Marriage and Society*, ed. R. B Outwaithe, Europa Publications, London, pp.117-136.

16. Cf. *An Honourable Estate*, GS801, Church House Publishing 1988, pp.22,23.

17. Note, for instance, Touchstone (aside), in Shakespeare's *As You Like It*, III,iii, 80ff. '. . .he is not like to marry me well, and not being well married, it will be a good excuse hereafter to leave my wife. . . .Come sweet Audrey, we must be married or we must live in bawdry.'

18. See T. C. Smout, in Outhwaite, *op. cit.* pp.204-236.

19. Stone *op. cit* p.33 quotes from the debate; 'we have in this age got the better of this as well as a great many other superstitious opinions . . . to render Christianity consistent with common sense.'

20. Joan Perkin, *Woman and Marriage in 19th Century England*.

London 1989 p. 158ff, referring also to J. R. Gillis, *For Better, For Worse.* OUP N.Y. p.219.

21. One of the findings of Blumstein & Schwartz, in *American Couples*, cited in M.DiCanio, *Encyclopedia of Marriage, Divorce and the Family*, NY 1989 s.v.Couples

22. The phrase belongs to Clifford Longley, religious correspondent of *The Times*, writing on the subject in 1991.

THREE

Biblical Evidence

It is natural for Christians, faced with an ethical or pastoral problem, to ask themselves what Jesus would have done in the circumstances. Often that is a frustrating question, because the New Testament contains no direct evidence. With the matter of cohabitation, however, we are on surer ground. We can actually listen in on Jesus' conversation with a woman who was cohabiting.

Marriage and celibacy

Perhaps we should first pause, and look briefly at the wider context of the New Testament teaching on marriage and relationships. While Jesus regarded marriage highly, as a creation ordinance (Mark 10:6-9) he did not regard it as something essential for the responsible citizen in Israel. While it is not entirely correct to say that all Jews would marry – the Essenes apparently valued celibacy, and some of them at least practised it according to Josephus – it was expected that a Jewish man would seek blessing and fulfilment in marriage.[1] For Jesus, however, celibacy was an option which he held up by his example and his teaching as an equal calling within the kingdom of God. Chastity and virginity were to be given credit. The inability to marry might be something conferred on a person by circumstances. All such people should be valued and respected (Matthew 19:12). The avoidance of adultery, enjoined in the commandments, was not to be merely legal respect for another man's property, but heartfelt respect for a woman's person (Matthew 5:28). In quoting Genesis 2:24 Jesus highlights God's ideal in marriage, that the partners should be helpers who match each other, and form a bond of unity with each other.

Jesus also stresses that there can be bonds which are greater, in particular that created by membership in the kingdom of God both in this world (cf Luke 14:26) or the next, for marriage is not a state which will be significant in the next world (Luke 20:34-36).

These themes are picked up by the apostles in their letters. The (marriage)-bed is to be undefiled and marriage is to be honoured while adultery and *porneia* are under judgment (Hebrews 13:4).[2] Respect should be shown by husbands to their wives as fellow-heirs of the grace of life, while wives should accept their husbands' leadership and seek moral rather than cosmetic attractiveness; such conduct, which reflects some of the secular ideals of austerity, would win unbelieving men to the faith (I Peter 3:1-7). Paul takes a similar line, while highlighting the value of celibacy in the light of the crisis of the age (I Corinthians 7:25-31 in which he recognizes that Jesus did not legislate for every eventuality, but draws conclusions in the light of the circumstances he knew). He recognizes the power of the sexual drive, and also the ties and worries that marriage can bring, in a realistic way (Ch.7:1-9,28). He also denounces *porneia*, in this case sexual relations between a man and his step-mother (ch 5:1) or with a prostitute (ch 6:15ff). His use of Genesis 2:24 in this last case reveals an awareness of the emotional and personal effects even of casual intercourse – an awareness that is almost before its time.[3] Quite how much he understood in this connection is not clear. Was he simply reaffirming a theological truth, or was he aware of the ways in which one act of intercourse will bring back memories and provoke comparisons with a previous partner in ways which still keep links with him or her?[4]

What we cannot do from the New Testament is specify when and how a marriage began. In rural Palestine it was probably quite clear, with festivities such as mentioned in John 2 and some of the parables leading to the bride being escorted from her father's house to the groom's. They would have been betrothed some time before, but it was expected that she would go to her bridal bed a virgin. In the cities of the Roman empire, such as Corinth, it was not always so clear-cut, and we can perhaps sense Paul's difficulty in transposing the Lord's teaching for Jewish Galilee to the multicultural melting pot of Corinth, and a church torn by issues of asceticism, apocalypticism, and antinomianism (I Corinthians 7:10,12,25,40). What he does seem (by his repeated use of the phrase 'let them marry') to expect is that as yet unmarried Christians accepting the call to marriage would explicitly marry. How formal that ceremony would be, and whether the elders of the church were there as elders, we are not told. It is not till the second century that we find specific marriage blessings in the church's liturgy – but that is the earliest we read the details of any service. Paul's emphasis on his readers remaining celibate if that is their marital state at the time is in line with Jesus' teaching (cf. Matthew 19 above), but is perhaps exaggerated by his awareness of an impending (as he thought) Second Coming.

There is a further consideration before we look at Jesus' teaching in some detail. That is the Old Testament background, with which Jesus shows himself very familiar. He not only quoted Genesis 2:24, but showed himself aware of the OT concern for the social underdog – in particular the orphan and the widow, who were in Jewish society in a structurally weak position. Separated from her family of birth by marriage a widow was in danger of losing the support of her in-laws because of her bereavement. Though Moses' provision for a 'Bill of Divorce' did give some degree of protection (as did the institution of bride-price and dowry) to a wife, a divorcée would be in as weak a position as a widow, if not a weaker one. However, what Moses had regulated (in Deuteronomy 24:1ff.) as a restraint on current abuses in his place and time, had been taken by the time of the Second Temple as permission to divorce. Jesus went back to the principles of the OT law, rather than sticking on its surface.

The woman of Samaria

The story of his encounter with the 'Woman of Samaria' which is told in John ch.4 is usually taken, by evangelicals at least, to be a superb example of Jesus the 'personal evangelist' meeting the woman's needs by pointing her to himself as Messiah. That is no doubt a valid way of taking the story, and is not alien to John's intention in telling it. According to this interpretation the woman's isolation from the community is noted. She had been ostracized and driven to collect her water at the unsocial hour of midday, which the respectable women avoided because of its heat. Jesus arouses her interest in the water of eternal life, and then unerringly exposes her sin by asking to talk to her husband as well. Then, skilfully dealing with her 'red herrings', he reveals that he is the Messiah, and she is so impressed that she abandons her water jar to fetch her neighbours to meet him, demonstrating her new faith.

We are asked, in this use of the story, to note how Jesus was prepared to break with convention in talking with a woman, and crossing racial barriers to bring someone salvation. The story must, of course, be set in its social context, and Jews had no dealings with Samaritans. We are sometimes asked to note his use of a charismatic 'word of knowledge' in exposing her sins, and as the exposition goes on we feel we can almost hear Jesus tut-tutting as he lists how many husbands she had. It is a way of preaching from the text which I have used myself, to encourage Christians in talking to others about Christ, to highlight the need for repentance as well as belief in God, and to point up Jesus' insight and compassion.

There is a flaw in that interpretation, however. Jesus does indeed talk about her five husbands, and her present man, but does not say anything directly condemnatory. In this story there is in fact no mention of divorce (*pace* e.g. Cornes, p.390, who assumes five divorces), no 'Go and sin no more,' or even 'Repent and believe'. Insight and compassion, and self-revelation, are the order of the day. And the woman's reaction is not shame, guilt or subdued repentance, but apparently joy; 'See someone who told me all I ever did'. Indeed, it was presumably from her that John the Evangelist heard the details of the story in the two days that Jesus and his disciples spent in the town afterwards. Is this the reaction of someone whose shame and guilt is exposed, even if it is exposed to be forgiven? Or is it the reaction of someone who felt condemned for years by social conventions, and has at last met someone who understands without condemning?

Those who remind us of the social context of the story have missed a point. She was a Samaritan woman. The Samaritans, for all the bad press given them by orthodox Jews from Ezra onwards, were a group which used and tried to adhere to the Mosaic Law; indeed part of the woman's conversation hinges on their belief that they had got the Law right and the Jews had got it wrong at least over where God's one true Temple was to be. Mosaic law does not give the wife power to initiate a divorce. From surviving texts and usage it would seem that the Samaritans like the first-century Jews adhered to the ruling, and may indeed have required priestly permission before a divorce was valid. Perhaps then we have to assume that she was such a termagant, or had proved so unfaithful, that five husbands had put her away. I think not.

Try this reading of the story for size. For various reasons five men have in turn married the poor woman, some perhaps have died on her, others may have tired of her and used their prerogative to divorce her. Such divorces would give her a bad reputation, making her out to be the adulterous party (cf. Matthew 5:32) even if there was no truth at all in the suggestion, while the death of two or three husbands might well lead the superstitious – even her own family, perhaps – to think she was jinxed, or worse. Yet a woman alone in the ancient Near East was in a parlous state. We easily slip into the idea that she was a young and attractive woman. I suspect that that was not so. Unless her marriages had lasted an exceptionally short time with little interval between she must have been in her mid-thirties, which in those days was not young – and of course she was not getting any younger. With no Social Security to fall back on she was at the mercy of charity, or of any man who cared to take her on. That is what, I suggest, had happened. Someone had taken his chance, and was using her (perhaps primarily as a carrier of water) without even the decency to make an honest woman of her.

According to this reading Jesus was not saying, 'You wicked woman! The thirst in your life is caused by your sins, and the way to drink of eternal life is to turn your back on them and the guilt they bring' but rather, 'You poor woman! The thirst you feel is for a genuine security and respect from the man in your life, and from the community where you live, and as Messiah I have come to restore right relationships. You are the victim of others' sins, and as Messiah I want to correct their sin and restore your respect'. What he was saying when he asked her to fetch her husband (or 'man' – the Greek, and the Hebrew or Aramaic behind it covers both English meanings) was, 'I want to sort out your relationship with the man now in your life'.

Perhaps that overplays her innocence – after all, we all fall short of the glory of God – and her mistreatment by men. The point is, however, valid and this is a reading of the story which I believe does more justice to her perspective as a Woman and a Samaritan in the first century than does the modern reading of her as the merry widow or wanton divorcée.

And what does it say to us about cohabitation? We do not know the sequel to the story, except that the woman does appear to be reintegrated within her community before Jesus leaves. Perhaps all we can say is that it is not a story of Jesus' outright condemnation of the situation that the woman was in (as some have assumed) but of his readiness to start from where a person has got to in her life, and to move forward constructively from there. That is not as clear and definite an answer as some might like. Perhaps that is because we are used to looking simply for proof-texts as the biblical way of answering ethical questions, and also because we find it easier to criticize and condemn past sin than to move forward positively from an unsatisfactory starting point.

Texts, contexts and principles

Rightly used there is nothing wrong in proof texts. They can highlight a response more clearly than intricate argument or the consideration of a narrative. Jesus himself used them – sometimes 'straight' and sometimes, I suspect, tongue in cheek in the course of argument with those biased against him. A text has to be set in its context, of course. To give an example which is in itself controversial, St. Paul's 'Women should keep silence in Church', is only half a sentence, the remainder of which suggest that worship was being disordered by whispered questions about the meaning of the service or the sermon from women who had hitherto been kept in the dark and the background – *kinder* and *küche* yes, but not *kirche* or anything more public or educational. Lacking the experience and education of their menfolk, and tasting a legitimate and new-found freedom in Christ they were actually causing interruption where Paul wanted to see decency and order. His response was that they should ask for explanations when they got home from husbands who were now, by implication, to be open and informative in the right place.

This in turn needs to be interpreted by reference to the more general principles enunciated in Scripture (not just the earlier passage in I Corinthians 11 in which women clearly were speaking out in prayer and prophecy); 'In Christ there is no . . . male nor female . . .' 'Be subject to one another, out of reverence for Christ'; or even the more radical 'The sabbath was made for man, not man for the sabbath', – i.e. the law is there to help, not hinder people. We should also look for the trends which are begun within scripture. Where did the writer and his contemporaries start from as they tried to discover the mind of Christ and apply it to reshape the lifestyle they had known? Where did

Christ himself begin from as he taught his contemporaries and challenged them? Paul's, 'Wives, obey your husbands . . .' would have raised no eyebrows among his male readers, though it may have roused some sighs of despair among the women. When he went on to put that obedience in the context of 'Husbands, love your wives as Christ loved the church . . .' he was saying something far more radical and challenging. I sometimes think it was the first blast of feminism to hit the church! If that seems forced, look at the mutuality expressed in I Corinthians 7:3,4 in which husbands are told to fall in line with their wife's desires, and *vice versa*.

And then in their turn both the proof texts and the principles need to be vetted against what we know of Christ's attitudes and practices – and in this particular case we have already noted that even on the more traditional and 'strict' interpretation of John 4, Jesus shows a more relaxed and egalitarian attitude to women than his contemporaries, an attitude reflected in other narratives also and one which surprised his followers. This process will in its turn shed light on difficult or ambiguous texts.

Jesus, divorce and 'greater righteousness'

Thus in the discussion in Mark 10 about.divorce Jesus established the eternal ideal with reference to the creation ordinance of marriage. Most commentators set the question within the context of a debate between two famous rabbis – Hillel and Shammai – as to what the 'unseemly thing' was for which Moses had permitted divorce (Deuteronomy 24:1.). (Matthew in recording the discussion took it in this context.) In Mark at least Jesus places limits on divorce as strict or stricter than anything either of those two rabbis taught, while recognizing that because of men's hardheartedness Moses had insisted on a bill of divorce. That in itself had been a humanitarian measure, protecting women from the worst abuses of easy divorce.

But, I believe, Jesus took that humanitarian measure further. Jewish law, and rabbinic discussion centred on whether and in what circumstances a man could divorce his wife. It was in gentile Rome that women themselves could initiate the legal process of divorce, and many commentators have taken this as evidence that Mark, possibly writing for a Roman Christian audience, has adapted Jesus' original teaching to the needs of his local church. (In fact that need not be the case. The Jewish community in Egypt – far nearer to Jesus' location – apparently recognized a woman's ability to initiate a divorce; the reported setting of this teaching is Gentile territory, so the adaptation may be Jesus' own, in any case.)

But let us assume that Mark is actually reporting Jesus, not adapting him. What conclusion follows from that assumption? Normal Jewish parlance would not talk of man committing adultery against his own wife (only against another man whose wife he debauched), yet Jesus speaks of that offence. He takes the side of the scorned wife, and feels the offence that she suffers. A man cannot in Jesus' eyes plead the innocent party merely by virtue of his maleness and the legal rights that gave him.

But more than that; if, as his cousin St. John tells us (chap.2:25), he did not need anyone to tell him about a person, for he knew what was in the person, then he was prepared to look beyond the legal forms to the manoeuvrings going on in people's relationships. A Jewish woman might not in normal circumstances have the legal right to initiate divorce, but by her conduct or persistent pleas, or by an appeal to the courts, she could make her husband initiate it. She could not plead innocence by virtue of the legal niceties. (This may seem special pleading, but I have heard an anthropologist describing such machinations in relatively modern Saudi society, in which the wife has no legal right of divorce. It is also possible that one of the Samaritan forms for a bill of divorce recognizes that the wife may have agreed to the process, though she could not formally start it.) Jesus was going behind the legal form to the nuances of attitude and behaviour beyond it, and challenging the hardness of their inner hearts, rather than their cleverness in giving a legal definition of 'the unseemly thing'. Was this what he meant when he challenged his followers to practise a 'righteousness greater than that of the pharisees and lawyers'?

In the teaching recorded in Matthew 5:31f. Jesus also goes behind the legal form to the social consequences of a man divorcing his wife. A divorced wife is forced into adultery – relations with another man in or out of marriage – since she would lack other means of support. Or (to take the slightly difficult Greek in a more awkward way) she is made out to be an adulteress, unjustly. Either way, Jesus is siding with the woman who is the victim of the divorce. He is not *simply* saying, 'God's law is being broken, God's will is being flouted' (though he does imply such concern in referring back, in Mark 10/Matthew 19, to the creation ordinance). He is concerned that someone is being exploited; someone who is in a weak position in the community is being abused, and manoeuvred into a situation she does not wish on herself. He is applying the Old Testament principle of the 'widow and the orphan'.

So where does the discussion get us? It does nothing to undermine the Christian ideal, set out in the creation ordinance, of lifelong monogamous marriage. Without actually saying that Moses was wrong to make provision for men's hardheartedness Jesus sets out the higher ideal, such that his followers (according to Matthew 19:10) recognize that the ideal is higher even than the strict Shammai's, and are shocked into questioning the risk of marriage at all (so Cornes, p.220f. citing others.) He states that people should not break up the institution that God has knit together – should not, mark you, not 'cannot'. The verb is jussive, not indicative or linked to an auxiliary verb 'can', while the object appears to be a thing (Greek. *ho*), not people – the couple – (which would be *hous*) as the BCP wrongly translates. In other words, Jesus is not saying divorce is a logical impossibility because marriage is indissoluble; he is saying that people can choose to divorce, but in doing so they break the commandment and sin against the other parties involved and against God.

What he calls for is, however, a righteousness that is greater than that of the scribes and pharisees; which goes to the heart of those sins and recognizes the hurt done to the other parties; which is not content to remain with a discussion of matrimonial causes, but is prepared to avoid injury to the vulnerable. He has come to 'fulfil the law' not destroy it or set aside its smaller points; while not wanting to abolish tithes of mint and cumin he is more concerned with the weighty matters, the glory, of the law which we might understand as its foundational principles (Matthew 23:23).

I shall be considering elsewhere (chapter 7) whether modern divorce law can match the spirit of such teaching, even if in the letter it appears to dispense with it.

The general questions raised by this discussion can be applied to cohabitation – or rather they can be asked of cohabitant couples. What Jesus exposes as wrong is the manipulation of one party to the marriage by the other – whether it is the socially 'weak' woman driving her husband to divorce, or the man, with power in the marriage because of the social structures of the day, treating his wife as a chattel to be disposed of at will, whatever the moral and social consequences for her. God's will is the moral and emotional unity of the couple, expressed in the phrase 'one flesh' – one lasting common bond of human sympathy. If the letter of the law, ancient or modern, preserves and encourages that, then thank God for his gift of the law; if the letter of the law can be manipulated to enable exploitation, then a higher righteousness is called for instead.

So we may ask the modern institution of marriage whether it of necessity oppresses (and some feminist writers have said that it does) and we may with more justice ask each husband and each wife whether they enjoy the looked-for common bond of human sympathy in their married life, or whether the one or the other is being used.

Cohabitation and the biblical portrait of marriage

We may also look at cohabitation, and ask whether as an

institution – as a regular pattern of behaviour – it leads inescapably to the abuse of one or both parties. The risk is perhaps greater than with conventional marriage, which is why I want greater legal recognition for the status to make abuse more difficult, but I do not believe that it is inevitable. We may therefore ask each cohabitant couple how closely their relationship matches the bond which is God's ideal or whether there is an element of manipulation there. I suspect that most relationships, both married and cohabitant, will turn out to be wanting to some degree under this scrutiny.

Later in this book I shall be suggesting that in limited circumstances a cohabitant couple have a relationship which ought to be given the respect of a marriage. If that is true in Christian terms, as well as on a secular, sociological level, we need to compare such a relationship with the pictures of marriage held up for us in the Bible. That may seem a clumsy way of phrasing what I wish to attempt, but very often biblical teaching about marriage comes as a spin-off from teaching about something else, notably about the relationship between God and Israel or God and the Church.

The key image is in Ephesians chapter 5, which is a complex double metaphor. Christ's love for the church is illustrated with reference to a husband's love for his wife, while wife and husband are challenged to live up to that illustration in their love for each other.

Paul's metaphor was not a new one. Hosea and later prophets had drawn the analogy between God as husband and Israel as wife, all too often as faithless wife. God's loyalty to his spouse, and his desire to call her back to the home where she belongs, is the recurring theme. This in turn leads to a picture of forgiving love, since Hosea's wife, like God's Israel, wanders off after strangers. Neither Hosea, nor the God whom his love reflects, stands upon the letter of the law. He maintains his covenant-love despite his partner's flouting of it. No divorce papers are to be found, for all the unseemly things that Israel has done (Isaiah 50:1) God bears the hurt, and in a sense 'gives himself up for her' as he continues to 'love and cherish her'.

I believe that when Malachi (in chapter 2:10-16), over three hundred years after Hosea, also talks about marriage he is taking up the same image – from the opposite side. Here it is the husband who is told that he must by loyal. He should not tire of his wife as she ages. The covenant made between husband and wife is one that should be kept, just as God has remained loyal to Israel. He should not do violence to his marriage pledge. It has bound her in companionship to him. (Malachi has used a word which is in the feminine form unique in biblical Hebrew. Is he hinting that a man should find in his wife the comradeship he would normally have looked for among other men?[5])

It is unlikely that Paul would have had texts of Hosea or Malachi unrolled before him as he wrote Ephesians. He would have had to rely on memory of what he had heard read and discussed. But his discussion in Ephesians 5 is very much in this tradition. The same limitations of writing 'technology' deprived him of the decisive paragraphs which we read in our Bibles. Thus his chapter 5:22 needs to be read as part of a flow of ideas running from far earlier in the letter. It is not the first thought he has had about husbands and wives, but the application to husbands and wives of the thought that includes chapter 5:1, 'Be imitators of God'. . . as Hosea was an imitator of God in forgiving and taking back his Gomer. Paul's thought, grammatically as well as logically, includes verse 21, Be 'subject to each other out of reverence for Christ.' The mutual respect which all Christians, male or female, bond or free, should show each other should be carried over into marriage, just as Malachi had spoken of the mutual comradeship of marriage.

Paul's thought progresses, however. Hosea's imagery had been of Israel the wayward wife. Malachi's strictures had been against the erring husbands of Israel. Paul is writing to a community whose relationship to God is fresh and new. They have not yet lost their first love. The church, therefore, is not the wayward wife, but the spotless bride. Within the church, however, old ideas have been carried over. When I read this passage at a wedding I sometimes feel embarrassed. It seems so condescending to the wife, as she is talked about rather than addressed directly for all but one of these eleven verses. 'He who loves his wife loves himself' does not sound a very romantic motive for married love. But Paul is putting some effort into remedying a fault which he perceived in man/woman relations in the church, and the wider society, of his day. The men needed to be persuaded that the Christian ideal of mutual respect was practical sense. Just as later Christians argued against slavery on the grounds that it was economically dysfunctional as well as morally unjustifiable, so Paul is telling those whose chauvinism will undermine the Christian pattern of marital relations that they are being impractical, not merely conservative.

This is why I believe the criticism of Paul as himself a chauvinist is misplaced. Perhaps later moralists have found that it suited them to focus on his 'wives obey your husbands'. He himself, I believe, focused on 'Husbands love your wives as Christ loved his bride,' and went on to argue why. His concern was not simply to be for the wife's moral purity (so Cornes p.75) which could become a form of social control, but also for her personal integrity and wholeness, just as Christ's creation of the church nurtured not just a legally moral community but a fellowship of those who had grown together into a mature humanity which reflected his human wholeness. (chapter 4:15f).

Though I do not wish to argue my case about cohabitation on these grounds, it is appropriate to note that in Paul's Greek the words for 'husband' and 'wife' are the normal words for 'man' and 'woman'. They do not in themselves imply that a public rite of passage – a marriage ceremony – had taken place. No doubt in most cases it had, but all that is demonstrable from the text is that each man and woman addressed would recognize that they belonged to each other (so verses 22,33).

Quality at the Heart of Christian Marriage

I have suggested that Paul's argument in Ephesians 5 is

essentially pragmatic and ethical, without being narrowly moralistic. Thus I find the use of this passage in particular to suggest that marriage is a 'sacrament' in the later sense to be misplaced. The Vulgate translation of 'mysterion' in verse 32 was sacramentum, which gives a superficial rightness to the suggestion. Marriage is no more a sacrament in the ecclesiological sense than the sunrise or a storm of rain which benefit just and unjust alike, though all three are pointers to God's love and character. The quirk of translation has turned a simile about God's love for the church, based on a 'momentous hidden meaning' (so mysterion . . . mega . . . verse 32) in Genesis 2:24, into dogma.[6] There is nothing magical about marriage as an institution in itself, though what each couple make of it can be pure magic, and in that is a portrait of God's love. And if the couple want to make magic together, let them look at God's love in Christ as their inspiration.

But is it an essential part of that portrait that the couple should be formally married? In Paul's argument it is the quality of the relationship which is at stake, rather than its formal beginning. He does, however, use imagery which draws upon marriage ceremonies in both Greece and Jewish Palestine in his day, perhaps correlating their ritual bathing in his mind with baptism. Perhaps we should admit that he presumes some form of marriage arrangement, but that may be because of the baptismal link. That does not mean, however, that the arrangements made by every one of his correspondents in Ephesus were the same, would have matched the details of the analogy, or would match what we expect in a modern marriage ceremony. Some details, such as a written contract, might well be more rigid than we would expect or even allow.

I began this chapter by suggesting that Christians, faced with a pastoral or ethical issue, would naturally look to the Bible for teaching and examples. Such a reaction is I believe basically correct, but can be misleading. We should not just look for the concordance references to the particular issues. We should ask: what are the underlying Christian principles which illuminate the straight instruction? Given that a particular course of action has been wrong – sinful – how should we move on from where it has landed us?

In making that point I have already assumed one principle, which may not be generally accepted. That is that we should be looking forward, not back. It is a principle which I have detected in Jesus' dealings with the Samaritan woman. It is even clearer, I think, in John chapter 8:1-12 where he deals with the woman caught in adultery. The punch line of the story is 'Go, sin no more' looking to the future, as much as Jesus' refusal to condemn her for past action. This is in keeping with the paramountcy of forgiveness in Jesus' dealings with people, even in areas where he could be strict in his general teaching. John 8:1ff. was the story that could not be lost from his followers' memories, even though they also remembered his exposure of the adultery of the heart in Matthew 5:27ff. It is in keeping with this principle of grace and acceptance that Paul emphasizes 'forgiving one another as Christ forgave you' to the Colossians. In Philippians he expresses how it works out in his own life: 'forgetting what lies behind and straining forward to what lies ahead I press on towards the goal . . .' (Philippians 3v13). This does not lead him to an amoral life, but to one which is not bowed down by judgement (I Corinthians 4:4) while being directed by Christlike standards.

There is a tension in this. We saw it in the teaching and practice of Christ himself in connection with adultery. It is, of course, the well-known tension between law and grace. Those who grasped the principle of grace alone received Paul's criticism: 'Let us continue in sin, that grace may abound? "God forbid!" Yet it would seem that he himself had been accused of this teaching. (Romans 6:1f.) Thus we see in his writing, and in that of his probable associates, a firm statement of a high sexual morality in connection with marriage; 'the . . . adulterers . . . will not inherit the kingdom of God' (I Corinthians 6:9f.). But the dots are equally important in that quotation. Idolatry, theft and greed, drunkenness and a sneering disposition are condemned equally with immorality, adultery and homosexual practice. Sexual sins need to be seen in proportion, even if they are easier to detect than greed or gluttony. Or 'Let marriage be held in honour among you all, and let the (marriage)-bed be undefiled, . . .' (Hebrews 13:4 – again other sins are listed. For the record, the word 'marriage' is not written in the Greek, but is implied by the sense.) Like Paul, those who take the principle of grace as the controlling principle in their understanding of Christianity need to beware of its inherent dangers. If I show grace in the way I deal with divorcés or cohabitants, I need to beware that I do not create excuses which cause 'a little one to stumble'. (Matthew 18:6, cf. Matthew 5:19.) I am aware of this danger, and suppose that a healthy respect for it leads many Christians to cling to the marriage morality that they know.

At times the New Testament is very basic and straightforward. Whatever rites (or absence of rites) had led each Christian couple into their relationship, Paul and his fellow apostles are as clear as the original Ten Commandments that adultery had no place amongst God's people, whatever their conduct before conversion (Ephesians 2:3). No one can justify sexual sin or any other form of sin, like backbiting or gluttony on the grounds that it gave God the opportunity to be more forgiving. (Romans 6:1-2.)

Whatever teaching the modern church gives in connection with marriage or cohabitation needs to retain this tension, even if it leads to the accusation that we are soft on sin. We offer the blessings of the high moral standard set by Christ, but we offer those blessings as an opportunity for the future, rather than as a source of mere condemnation for the past. We also need to maintain the New Testament proportion; acquisitiveness receives equal condemnation with immoral sexual behaviour and robbery, and its antidote is a Godlike generosity. (Ephesians 4:28.)

Notes

1. For a summary of rabbinic views on marriage, see for example Wm. Barclay's commentary on Matthew in the Daily Study Bible series, under Matthew 19:1-12.

2. *Porneia* is a difficult word to translate. In some places it means specifically prostitution, as in I Corinthians 6:16 referred to below. Elsewhere it means any sexual sin, as in I Corinthians 5:1 where the actual fault is incest. Thus it can mean fornication; sex-outside-marriage, but that begs the question of what entailed marriage. In the passages of Paul and Peter quoted here the Greek words for husband and wife are the normal words for man and woman, occasionally qualified by the possessive adjective meaning 'his/her own', 'his/her proper' . . . *idios*. Neither Paul nor Peter specify how they knew they were proper to each other, and as we saw in discussing Roman marriage law, there were many routes to such commitment, not all formal public ceremonial. Where Paul does make reference to the law of marriage – as an illustration in Romans 7:1-6 addressed to a mixed Jewish and Gentile-Christian audience – it is either to the most strict (and rarest) form of Roman marriage, or to Jewish law as interpreted by Christ (not Hillel or Gamaliel his grandson, Paul's tutor) that he appeals. In this only death can dissolve the marriage bond.

3 I owe the observation that Paul was ahead of his time in recognizing the psychological impact of intercourse to Cornes, *Divorce and Remarriage*, London 1993 p.68, citing Barrett and others. This verse does not mean that intercourse itself creates a marriage. Paul is saying that the bond thus created is an illegitimate and immoral one, and that Christians should flee it (verse 18). Christians who use the passage to argue that intercourse makes a marriage have totally overlooked its context. The point is that bonds are created in this case which conflict with the bonds between the Christian and Christ. What might be argued, however, in the light of the often very informal beginnings of *contubernia* in Roman lower class society, is that intercourse with the intention of a stable relationship would confirm the couple's intention, and form a bond between them. But that is not what Paul is actually talking about here.

4. This point is further discussed in Tim Stafford's *Sexual Chaos* Leicester 1993 p.110f. He writes as if Paul knew all the psychology.

5. Baldwin also suggests this (TOTC *in loco*) and sees in the textual difficulties at this point the interference of copyists who did not like the Malachi's strictness – or his apparent disagreement with Deuteronomy. *Haggai, Zechariah, Malachi,* Tyndale Press, London (Leicester) 1973.

6. Cornes (p.77f.) is helpful, here. See also my *Marriage before Marriage?* p.16.

FOUR

Christian Ideals

O nce upon a time there was a couple who loved each other, and were considering marriage. Because of their own family background it was very much the Christian picture of marriage that they looked at, and what they saw impressed them, but daunted them. They were, they felt, unworthy of the high ideals presented to them and felt unable to live up to those ideals. They chose as a result not to marry but to live together, since that presented demands that they felt they could attain. It was some years ago that I was told about them, and I do not know whether or not their story has ended happily ever after.

But what was the ideal which they looked at and felt overawed by? There are many facets to the jewel that is Christian marriage, and over the years the light has reflected off different faces. Was it the high ideal of companionship within the covenant that the couple make with each other? Was it the sacramental permanence and portrait of God-like love which daunted them? Was it the earthy honesty which spoke of the joy of their bodily union, or the austere asceticism which viewed marriage as a protection against the lusts of the flesh? Were they misled by the distortion so easily read into the bride's promise to obey in some of our services? And were there features of the Christian message that they had overlooked, because they are not usually spoken of in the same breath as marriage? In the first flush of engagement it is not done to think about things which might need forgiveness, though in practice the couple may already be learning much about it through their relationship. These features are all part of the ideal in Christian marriage, and though they may seem contradictory at times, are facets of the same gem.

Marriage: a vision to claim

That gem is precious, and is to be held up to couples considering marriage, to couples caught up in cohabitation, and to
those already committed in marriage. But it is not merely an
ideal to hold up for admiration, or to turn away from sorrow-
ing. It presents us with a measure against which each relationship can be tested, whether a marriage or a cohabitation. It
also contains the promise of grace to live up to it, for it is
offered to us by God as an option to choose and aspire to,
rather than as a mirage to tantalize and betray us. I believe that
the most significant part of the Anglican marriage services is
the blessing that comes after the promises and before the
prayers. (Section 19, Alternative Service Book p.293.) That is
not because I reckon a priestly blessing makes the whole affair
sacramental – if it is a sacrament then it is the couple who are
priests for the day, consecrating their relationship by word and
action. It is because the message of that blessing is this: *God is
on your side and wants your marriage to go well; all the
promises of Christianity that God is present with us, that his
grace can strengthen and guide us morally and can enable us to
understand, forgive and grow in maturity, are as true in the setting of your marriage as in all life, as is the assurance that even
failure holds within it the seeds of restoration and renewal.* The
service is saying: *all this can be yours,* and the blessing affirms
this is what God wants for you.

So what are the characteristics of 'Christian' marriage which
we hold up for people to opt into? The features which I listed
earlier have all in one generation or another been highlighted
by Christian teachers. Some of them may seem to twentieth
century Christians to be strange versions, or even distortions, of
the truth. Perhaps that is because we notice the highlights most
readily, and forget to see what was in the shadows behind
them. What follows is not an attempt to describe the development of Christian ideas about marriage in full. It is more like a
series of stills from a film, picking out significant points, rather

than running the whole sequence.

As we have seen, Augustine held that the procreation of children was the great purpose of marriage, one of the 'goods' that lay at its heart. While he could see in Genesis chapter 1:28 the divine command to be fruitful and multiply as the first command (and also the first blessing) to humankind, he was also subject to the personal and corporate anxiety of his class in the later Roman empire – lest there should be no children to carry forward the family name, continue to pray (with pagan or Christian prayers) at the family mausoleum, and maintain the Roman tradition. This view of child-rearing was coloured, too, by a Christian ideal that children might be born who should be born again to the greater glory of God through the faith. (*De nuptiis et concupiscentia* I,iv ff., I,xvii.) These ideals of fertility and faith are reflected in the prayers of the Anglican marriage services, ancient and modern.

Augustine was not simply a child of his time. Secular Rome set so great a store on child-bearing that the failure to bear a child might be a ground for divorce. The debate was to continue (at least among the landed classes and nobility) well into the middle ages – often couched in terms of annulment on the alleged grounds of non-consummation. Augustine recognized the argument, but rejected it. The oath (*sacramentum*) of marriage forged a permanent bond, which could not be set aside (*De nuptiis* . . . I,x). Thus, while for mediaeval and later lawyers deliberate refusal to consummate a marriage may be grounds for annulment, the inability to bear or father children is not[1]. Neither is the choice not to have children, though I believe that such a choice is not one to be made hastily or without deep thought, unless there is some genetic or other medical reason for restraint. There may be a case for deferring child-bearing for a while, not least to give time for a couple to know each other more closely. If nothing else a positive decision not to have children should be strong enough to survive the regrets of a lonely old age.

Self control and self-surrender

Two strands of thought came together in Augustine's thinking about sexual relations. One was derived from those classical philosophers who regarded it as evil to have lost rational control of oneself. For them passion was the great disaster, meaning not simply deep emotion, such as anger or love as with us, but irrational action or feelings because the self comes to be controlled by the force of such emotions. The words *passio* and *pathos* have the basic meaning of suffering, being on the receiving end, and so losing control. The other strand was more purely biblical. Shocked, perhaps, by the licence of the big cities of the Roman Empire the writers of the New Testament letters had denounced lust and sexual immorality roundly. Such conduct would not lead anyone into the kingdom of God. They were conscious, too, of the urgency of the times, anticipating an imminent tribulation and subsequent return of the Lord. In that setting, Paul had suggested, marriage itself might be a distraction from the more important business of Christian life and service, though recognizing the potency of human sexuality he had acknowledged that it was better to marry than to burn (I Corinthians 7:9).

With a less immediate sense of the Second Coming, later generations of Christians read the Apostles' hesitancy and caution about marriage in the light of the very obvious evils of lust, attacked in the New Testament and visible all around them in late Roman civilisation. Thus it became clear to them that Paul in I Thessalonians 4:4 had been talking about taking a wife (*skeuos* – 'vessel') without lust or *passio*, rather than a man's sexual self-control generally (cf. Augustine, *De nuptiis* . . . I.iv). In this atmosphere celibacy could become an end in itself, a means of avoiding contamination, as much as a means by which a person was freed to serve the kingdom of God more wholeheartedly. For Augustine the argument became more complex, because of his consciousness of original sin and his consequent arguments with Pelagians who accused him of treating God's good gifts as evil. Indeed, he seems to an observer looking back on the debate, to have come within a hair's-breadth of such a statement. 'All that comes of concubinage (in this context he seems to mean intercourse) is lust' (*De Nuptiis . . I.x*). But Augustine's arguments have been exaggerated by his desire to demonstrate that mankind is not now free to determine his own good conduct, but is depraved and needs God's grace to achieve anything, even the good things of marriage (*De Nuptiis . . . I.xvii*).

Taken out of this polemic context and the forceful language that it provoked, Augustine's support for marriage seems somewhat grudging, and his arguments at times forced. But he was aware from his own life as much as from what he saw around him that men could be very lustful, that sexual drives could hold people in thrall, and that lack of self-control could be very destructive – even though it may seem to twentieth century eyes that his own cool calculations before conversion, over his concubine and his impending marriage, had lacked integrity.

Augustine's second benefit in marriage was *fides* – often rendered fidelity, but having a wider meaning covering loyal relationship. He regarded this too as a natural good, admired even among pagans. Surrounded by the dangers of lust, marriage seemed a protection against those evils, and fidelity within it a source of security. There might be here the germ of the idea captured in modern writing about marriage by the word covenant, but if challenged Augustine would have denied that one could expect in marriage quite the comradeship one would find with a like-minded male friend.

It was along the lines of protection from sin that thought about the good things of marriage developed, so that by the time of Cranmer's prayer books marriage could be spoken of as a 'remedy against sin, to avoid fornication, that such persons as be married might live chastely in matrimony and keep themselves undefiled members of Christ's body'. (BCP 1549 with modern spelling – 1552 rephrased it as 'such persons as have not the gift of continency . . . '.)

It is easy to smile at this sixteenth-century language, and the fifth-century thinking that ultimately lies behind it. We do not by and large have the same dread of sin that our ancestors did, and the late twentieth century Western vision of sexual love is shaped (or marred) as much by Marie Stopes, D.H. Lawrence and Hugh Heffner as by a fear of Pelagius. Many Christians have looked back to the frank delight expressed in Genesis 2: 23, or the Song of Songs, as well as the dire warnings of Ephesians 5: 3ff. Thus the ASB marriage service seems to contradict Cranmer with its language of the 'joy of their bodily union' though that perhaps echoes the wife's promise in the mediaeval Sarum rite to be 'buxom in bed and at board'.[2]

But before we dismiss Cranmer's austerity out of hand we should pay heed to it. To be offered a remedy against sin is no light blessing. To dismiss all God-given sexual desire as lust, and all passion (in the ancient or modern sense) as improper, is perhaps overenthusiastic sin-hunting. To recognize that those sexual appetites are strong and that passion and feelings alone do not justify a person's actions or relationships is wisdom. To deny that there is a great deal of selfishness, self-gratification and inhuman treatment of other people that goes on under the fair-sounding guise of love or freedom and independence or experience or self-discovery is self-deception. Humankind can be most inhumane to its kind and can benefit from any institution which remedies those sins. Mutual and exclusive trust, expressed in explicit consent and vouched for by witnesses, is the proper setting within which sexual passion should be enjoyed. To submit to that discipline is in fact a gift of freedom and security. Within that trust there is the opportunity for self-giving love which may take time to find its fullest and richest expression. Without it the restraints on selfishness are minimal. In this sense we should be saying that marriage offers a remedy against sin, though in honesty we cannot say that it guarantees a cure.

Sin, slavery and commitment

I believe, however, that we can extend what we understand by a remedy against sin beyond that. It is not simply sexual sins for which it can be a remedy, but more widely the sins of exploitation and abuse between man and woman, and woman and man. Feminist writers have with some justification pointed to the ways in which the institution of marriage has enslaved women, at times keeping them under the control of father or husband, and offering them no other trade than housewifery.[3] But while exposing the abuses they have overlooked the restraint which recognized marriage, and restriction of divorce or dismissal at will, has imposed on the casual exercise of male dominance.

Liz Hodgkinson, who suggests that 'as marriage laws have become more codified women have lost all their rights,' also admits that since the beginnings of sexual liberation in the 1920s women have become even more imprisoned.[4] 'What really needs to be changed,' she goes on, 'is the way in which men and women see each other. They must stop regarding each other as possessions, accept each other as individuals, and let each other remain so'. She then suggests that non-intimate friendships, like brother and sister, are the way forward, which I think is less than realistic; sexual appetites and sexual bonding are strong, even if there is a right place for brother/sister-like relationships. But what she has upheld as the needed change is surely contained in the picture of marriage upheld by St.Paul in Ephesians 4 and 5. I say in chapter 4 as well as 5 because that chapter emphasizes the growth to maturity which Christians want to see in each other as they imitate Christ – a growth which is the background to what is said about marriage in chapter 5 and which, *pace* Hodgkinson, does involve interdependence and support and encouragement.

It may seem an unfair argument for me to contrast an ideal picture of marriage with Hodgkinson's grim portrait of the reality that can exist, but she is doing the same in reverse; holding the distorted reality which is what people make of marriage against her idealized picture of non-intimate friendship. She criticizes the institution and suggests its abandonment. I acknowledge the criticism in part, but suggest that even when faulted it still offers protection against worse uncertainties and abuses. In the context of cohabitation I recognize that some of the constructive freedoms of which she speaks can be found among such relationships, but believe that they lack the built-in remedy for sins of abuse. Since each couple are making their own rules (or think they are) they may build in the abuse rather than the safeguard whether it be against infidelity, exploitation, or brevity and lack of commitment.

The third of Augustine's benefits of marriage supplies that lack. He speaks of marriage as a *Sacramentum* – a soldier's oath of allegiance to his general, validated and hallowed by imprecation to the gods and not to be broken. We noted in the last chapter how it had been used to translate the Greek *mysterion* in Ephesians chapter 5 in accordance with its secondary meaning of sacred and secret rite. I propose to distinguish the Latin word in what follows from the English word sacrament which enshrines within it connotations of a further thousand years of discussion to which Augustine was not party. The stress in Augustine's teaching was that here is a holy bond that cannot be dissolved by human whim or action. Again in *De nuptiis* (I.xvii) he argues that neither divorce nor the adultery which perhaps preceded it actually breaks the bond of marriage. For him even the Matthean exception left a bond, even if a legal divorce did take place.

Roman law saw consent as the key feature of marriage, though because of the various strata of Roman society and the private nature of such relationships, that consent was at times lightly given and lightly taken back. Augustine and others before him, by classing that consent on the level with an oath of allegiance had given it a degree of certainty, reinforced by the public, or at least communal, authority of the church which it had previously lacked. Thus two hundred years before him we can see in the arguments between Hippolytus and Pope Callistus evidence that the Roman church urged marriage *kata nomon* – according to law or to custom (*nomos* can mean either) – on anyone seeking baptism into the faith, but also treated the legally dubious cohabitation (*contubernium*) between a slave and a free person (for Hippolytus, only between a slave girl and her master) as a marriage which held all the permanency the church could give it.[5]

This, of course, given the hardness of men's hearts, did not settle the matter, and mediaeval church lawyers debated at length on behalf of their powerful patrons on the nature of the sacrament, and on who might be excused the rigours of the doctrine because of some obscure and hitherto unremembered cousinage. Into this discussion a subtle change was introduced, again by means of the double sense of a Latin word, so that affection as well as intention (both *affectio*) came to be seen as a central good in marriage. Thus Cranmer can choose as his third purpose for which matrimony was ordained not sacramental permanence as such, but mutual society in prosperity and adversity. The permanence is physical rather than metaphysical. What is on offer is a quality of relationship which reflects the divine commitment to mankind (as St. Paul had argued) but it is seen in practical terms in the commitment of the couple to each other when things are difficult for them.

If human marriages have failed to live up to that, and if the institution of marriage in England today is being whittled away until the minimal contractual commitment is to one year before a divorce unless very grave and dangerous circumstances warrant speedier dissolution, what chance is there for a relationship that does not have the public support and spiritual backing of a *sacramentum* – a vow in church or even a pledge before a registrar? In purely statistical terms, it has perhaps half as good a chance. Yet that still means for some cohabiting couples, I suggest, that there is a degree of permanence and commitment which (if our English marriage laws were not so restrictive) would be given the credit of matrimony.

The meaning of love

While our Anglican services have retained the neat liturgical pattern of three 'causes for which matrimony was ordained,' we have adapted the three considerably. Thus mutual society help and comfort have become the practical expression of the *sacramentum* while for some the sacrament is enshrined in the priest's presence and blessing, or the couple's promises or perhaps their action in consummating the marriage. Those words have been adapted further in the modern services to be the first, rather than the last of the good things of marriage, and to include again the idea of faithful commitment. This change of order reflects the changing emphasis in marriage. Affection there was (in the modern sense) in ancient marriages, but it was not part of the ideology of marriage in the way it now is. It would often be the consequence of a marriage arranged for other reasons, dynastic or financial. While in societies where the groom might actively court his bride there would be an element of mutual liking in the arrangement, other factors would predominate initially. 'Companionate marriage' is a relatively modern ideology.[6]

That does not mean that love in marriage is a modern idea, Cranmer's service asked the couple 'wilt thou . . . love, honour and keep . . . ?' This, of course, reflected St Paul's teaching in Ephesians and Colossians. What is perhaps modern is the understanding that is put on love by those who speak those promises. So easily it seems that we are speaking of romantic or emotional or even sexual love as the words trip off the tongue during the service. It is right that those feelings should be involved in the service and the celebration. It would be unnatural to exclude them, given the myths that have been woven round the marriage day by popular culture in magazines, stories, and gossip. It is important, however, in an age when permanence and commitment seem to be dirty words in many areas of life, for the couple to realize that their promise to love is a moral commitment, given in response to a command. It is an act of the will, not a biochemical response over which they have no great control. It is not merely a description of their current feelings for each other projected into the future, though marriage is not an excuse for the care and respect which is expressed in the romance of courtship to cease.

When St. Paul instructed husbands to love their wives the word he used was the standard Christian word for love, *agape*, which seems to have been adopted by the early church as the best way of expressing the qualities they looked for in love. In non-church Greek it is a far rarer word, with the connotation of caring concern, showing itself in practical ways. That was what the church wished to denote when it spoke of love, and that is what should be seen in Christian married love too, alongside the other elements of emotion and sexuality. It is a moral quality as well as a romantic one. That means it is a conscious and deliberate choice, not a passion alone. Thus when the couple respond 'I will,' they are not saying 'that is what I am about to do. Get on with it!' They are saying, 'that is what I have deliberately chosen to do.' It is a moral commitment which will continue through all the seasons of life, in sickness as well as in health and not merely while the feeling lasts. Thus those who would put a gloss on the phrase in the service 'till death us do part', interpreting it as the death of the marriage, or the death of love, are distorting the promise. They may be realistic, and the moral strength to keep the vow may turn out to be lacking, but that is not what the words mean. The promise is to act caringly, even if the emotions have been numbed by crying children or the passage of years.

Once again we may ask, are such qualities uniquely to be found within a marriage that has been undertaken in church or even before a registrar? It is perhaps true that there is a strength in the institution and the public commitment it involves which catches the couple up in something that they recognize as bigger than themselves, and which will give an added strength to their commitment when things are difficult in their relationship. If so, it could be argued that anything that undermines the institution, such as easier divorce, is in fact reducing the structural support it gives to each couple. The prevalence of cohabitation may also work this way, as married couples feel they can behave as if they were merely cohabitants, finding it easier to walk away. Conversely, to give greater recognition to cohabitation, making it less easy to walk away from, may serve to strengthen the institution of marriage. Either way, Christians hold up to those who marry the possibility of enriching and developing each other's character and self through such a covenant to love and cherish.[7]

God's hand in marriage

I have already suggested that a couple may have learned something about mutual forgiveness in their relationship, even before marriage, and also that what Paul wrote about married love in Ephesians 5 needs to be interpreted in the light of what he says about Christian life as a whole in Ephesians 4: 15-32. Perhaps marriage is in a sense sacramental, in that it can demonstrate the Godlike qualities of acceptance and tolerant understanding. But does it happen *ex opere operato*? – just because the words are said? I prefer to work Paul's analogy (chapter 5:32) the other way; we can draw on the Christian graces of forgiveness and patient love in order that the natural good of marriage may be enriched and preserved. The shape of the service itself becomes a message. Daunting commitments are followed by the assurance of God's support, after which the couple move forward to the communion rail to pray, symbolizing their need for God's grace throughout their life together to support the promises they have made.

The ideal which Christians offer to couples in marriage is of permanent security and support 'till death do us part'. As if to reinforce that phrase the declaration that the couple are married is juxtaposed with the challenge 'those whom God has joined together, let no man put asunder'. The ASB correctly goes back to the original saying of Jesus, and has 'that which . . . ' but in doing so perhaps loses something of the liturgical and personal force of the words. Either way, what is being said is not simply a denial of the authority of divorce courts.[8] There were no such things in Jesus' day, anyway, and divorce was a matter for the husband (and in Samaria, perhaps, the high priest too). It is more like those general letters 'to whom it may concern'. The couple themselves are being told not to act in such a way as to break up their own relationship; their families – and the respective in-laws – are being warned not to disrupt the marriage, and to respect the couple's right to be together as their primary relationship, for a man leaves his father and mother to cleave to his wife; friends and future acquaintances are being warned off – these two belong together, and no one should come between them by seduction or slander. Their own children, in due time, must learn that their parents have to have time and space for each other, whatever their parallel duty to their offspring.

While this declaration in itself may not always be heeded it does sum up one of the things which a formal marriage does; it declares that the couple do belong to each other exclusively, for all to know. That is a feature which is lacking formally in a cohabiting relationship, though within a circle of friends and family such relationships will be known and recognized, however grudgingly, after a time.

This is the pattern of marriage which, to say the very least, Christians offer to couples for their good – for God's commands and patterns are intended as benefits for mankind. There have been times and places where an appearance of conformity to this standard has been maintained by society. Perhaps Britain in the early years of this century was one such place, which is why calls for 'traditional values in marriage' have a certain appeal. That is the tradition we grew up with. Whether the reality behind that appearance lived up to the Christian standard is a moot point. I have myself certainly heard anecdotal evidence from elderly parishioners both of abuse within marriage, and of stable cohabitation. What the Christian ideal also gives us is a yardstick against which marriage as an institution, and our individual marriages, may be measured.' That all marriages – even the 'good' ones – probably fall short of the ideal is a cause not for despair, but for renewed commitment.

I therefore find some encouragement in the prayers of the Book of Common Prayer marriage service. In these prayers Isaac and Rebecca, Abraham and Sarah, are cited as examples of faithful marriage. When we read the actual stories of these heroes and heroines of faith in Genesis we find that their relationships seem at times to have run anything but smoothly. If that were so, and God still was able to use and bless them, then we should not despair at our shortcomings.[10]

Notes

1. I speak as an Anglican. Some Roman Catholics have refused to marry paraplegics on the grounds that they are unable to consummate the marriage. That is taking the logic of defining marriage simply in terms of its constituent good parts to a sad extreme.

   Some mediaeval royalty allegedly remained celibate within their marriages – notably a Northumbrian queen (who possibly did not like the husband she had been matched up with) and Edward the Confessor. (Perhaps lesser folk did the same, but no one reported it.) Their action was linked up with the belief that any intercourse was inevitably corrupted by the sin of lust, an idea found in Augustine and earlier, and seemed to be canonized by the dogma of Mary's perpetual virginity.

2. There is some discussion of this in *Anglican Worship Today* (pp. 186-191) which was prepared in informal consultation with those who had written the service.

3. So Cicely Hamilton in 1909, cited by Liz Hodgkinson, *Unholy Matrimony* p. 93.

4. *op.cit.* p100.

5. cf. Ed. Dix & Chadwick, *The Treatise on the Apostolic Constitutions of St. Hippolytus of Rome*, London, SPCK 1968 p.xvii, & text xvi;6,7,23,24. Before we side with Hippolytus for the rigour of his morals we should realize that he is giving way to Roman prejudice against the slave class, and Callistus, the ex-slave, is applying consistently within the prevailing civil law the Christian teaching that male and female are equal before God, as are slave and free and freed and citizen.

6. Alan McFarlane, *Marriage and Love in England, 1300-1840*. Blackwell, Oxford & NY 1986, discusses this development at length. It is a complex issue, and literary evidence does not always mean what it seems. Does Langland's criticism of marriages for money represent a commonplace of his time, or a new thought in the light of the growing value placed on love? Does the 'courtly love' of the earlier middle ages represent a denial of marital fidelity, or the beginnings of romantic love as the basis of relationships? cf. S. Dixon, *The Roman Family* p.70.

7. The idea of developing in love through the stages of life is discussed, for instance, by Jack Dominian in *Marriage, Faith and Love*, DLT, London 1981.

8. The lawyer, John Bullimore, discusses how legal procedures can push couples asunder inadvertently, because of the way they are operated. *Pushing Asunder?*. Grove Books, Nottingham, 1981.

9. This approach is explored in relation to marriage and to cohabitation by Gary Jenkins in *Cohabitation: a biblical perspective*. Grove Books, Nottingham, 1992.

10. I have not referred to these stories and the marriage customs contained within them in the earlier chapter on the biblical teaching, because the customs and circumstances seem so different from our own. Also I suspect there was a great deal left to be understood by the hearers when the stories were first told. So the fact that Isaac simply 'took Rebecca to his tent' (Genesis 24: 67), implies not (as it might seem to us as we read the story) the absence of a formal marriage, but rather is a technical term for the wedding, just as for us to speak of 'giving away' a daughter does not mean a casual disposal. The Patriarch's marriages seem to have broken with contemporary custom in some respects. cf. K. Kitchen, *The Bible in its World*, Exeter 1977, p.69 f.

FIVE

Marriage: a Social Affair

Step we gaily, on we go,
   heel for heel and toe for toe,
arm in arm and row on row,
   all for Maire's wedding.

Over hill ways, up and down,
   myrtle green and bracken brown,
   past the sheiling, through the town,
   all for sake of Maire.

Red her cheeks as rowans are,
   bright her eyes as any star,
fairest o' them all by far
   is our darling Maire.

Plenty herring, plenty meal,
   plenty peat to fill her creel,
plenty bonny bairns as weel,
   that's our toast for Maire.*

It would be easy to assume that marriage is a relatively private affair concerned with the domestic and sexual arrangements between two individuals. Our twentieth century perception of the world is sufficiently individualistic for this kind of tunnel

---

*Though deriving from the west coast of Scotland, this song reflects the traditional country wedding over many parts of Britain. A similar village ritual is described in the nostalgia of *Hardy's Under the Greenwood Tree.*

vision to dominate, and restrict, the way people understand marriage. While this view is true it is not the whole truth. There are still a lot of familial and social transactions going on on the day, and marriage as an institution fulfils a number of functions within society. It is not, therefore, merely a 'licence to copulate', as the old jibe has it.

Society's interest in marriage

Both society and the narrower family therefore have an interest in whether couples marry formally, or sidestep that event. If they do sidestep the event, society may still legitimately claim an interest in their arrangements because of the way in which they affect those features of society that marriage would normally regulate – for instance inheritance after intestate death.

While the Christian 'goods' of marriage begin to affirm these wider functions in marriage, and while the liturgy hints at some of the transactions on the day, they do not exhaust the list by any means. An anthropologist observing both the institution and the event will want to add to the list considerably – and in fact there is an extensive literature on the subject. It draws on studies of many different cultures. In arguing whether a society could function without marriage anthropology drew up not so much a definition of marriage as a check-list of functions which marriage served. Where it found an institution around which those functions clustered, there it recognized marriage, and recognized it as a working institution even if conventional Western features were lacking.[1] For the record, conventional Western marriage now lacks some of the features on the check-list.

I believe that it is legitimate to adopt this functional approach in Britain today, and ask whether the practice of cohabitation has become a social institution which is definite enough to be recognized as one of the current forms of marriage. The fact that it is not recognized as such in law does not prevent us asking such a sociological question. A similar sociological approach to the institution of marriage itself will give an empirical picture which differs from the legal and ethical theory. I will argue also that it is not adequate ethically for Christians to say that the law of the land defines marriage for them. Just as they may ask whether cohabitation in general, or the behaviour of a cohabitant couple in particular, fulfils the moral or sociological criteria of marriage, they may wish to ask whether the legal forms of marriage or even the attitudes of a married couple match the ethical pattern they hold to. We shall therefore be juggling with several questions in the air at once.

The functions of marriage

Leach and Gough list the definitive functions of marriage. For an English context these may be summarized under six heads, to which I would myself add a seventh.

1. *It confers legitimacy on the children of the union. That is to say it is they who have the right to inherit status and property from the parties to the marriage.*
   English law is progressively removing the disabilities resulting from illegitimacy. For instance, since the Family Law Reform Act of 1987 an illegitimate child has rights of inheritance alongside legitimate children unless explicitly excluded in the deceased's will. This applies whether the child was openly acknowledged, or whether paternity was denied but proven. Though in some ways the Children Act of 1990 retains the difference between married and unmarried parenthood it makes the acceptance of parental responsibility more straightforward, while more recent legislation is attempting to enforce more rigorously the support of children by their parents, even when absent. In social terms the sad and bitter treatment given to illegitimate children just after the First World War, for instance, no longer applies. When one child in four in this parish, to give an example that is near at home, or one in three in Manchester comes from a single parent family,

parents can no longer call their children in (as elderly parishioners have described to me) to stop them playing with a 'love child'. I suggest therefore that in this point cohabitation and marriage are converging, though the distinction in law does still remain.

2. *Marriage confers control over (or at least a strong interest in) the fertility and sexual activity of the partners to the union to each other.*

Cohabitation confers no 'marital rights' as such, but the partners have an emotional and indeed a medical interest in each other's sexual activity. The hurt which follows infidelity may well lead to the same sense of outrage, betrayal and defilement as it would in formal marriage. In practice also the British courts have been responding to the pressure of women's groups in recognizing that 'marital rights' are not absolute even in marriage if a separation has taken place.

3. *It gives rights to the domestic and economic services of the spouses to each other, often within the setting of a wider kinship group.*

There is a quip, first put on paper by a disenchanted western feminist, Ann Oakley, that marriage begins when you sink into his arms, and ends with your arms in his sink. (I have heard it reversed, with 'her' substituted for 'his'.[2]) The balance of this domestic economy may not always be fair, as Oakley suggests, and this is especially so if a society has changed rapidly and radically. Thus (to generalize) in parts of rural Africa the men would not deign to get involved in the women's work of agriculture, and leave it to their wives, even though the traditional man's work of hunting has largely ceased leaving them without occupation. Similarly, in Western countries women can still be expected to manage the house despite a growing role in commercial or industrial activity outside the home. The 'new man' may acknowledge a wider role in the home, but the change in his role has not taken place so rapidly as that of his partner.

This particular point, however, does not invariably work against the wife. In a subsistence economy especially the sharing of each other's labour, and obligations to each other's kin focused on bride price, can give a promise of security, and be a defence for the wife against the casual breakup of the marriage and against the destitution that would follow this. Mutual gifts between the families, or a dowry, can mean the establishment of an economic base for the couple.

In some respects both cohabitation and marriage represent a sharing in the household economy, not least the sharing of the house itself, which makes up a considerable proportion of anyone's financial commitments. There can be economies of time and money in sharing household tasks and buying in greater quantities, even if the likelihood of couples working together in the same trade is perhaps less than in the distant past. In some respects a couple, married or not, will be treated alike by the state, for instance in connection with Social Security benefit. But since the 1988 Budget tax has been calculated separately even for married couples though the married status has been encouraged by means of a special allowance. How each couple manage their own finances during their marriage or partnership will vary though spouses can expect support as a right, but the rights of cohabitants to support from the partner in the event of a split, even if one has given up career prospects because of the relationship, are nil. Conversely, the late Community Charge enforced joint liability.

4. *Marriage could be a means of controlling or transferring property, or the rights to it , within the present generation, and . . .*

5. *. . . be a means of establishing a common fund of property to be passed on to the children, or retained within the wider family group.*

Prior to the Married Women's Property Act 1882 marriage was a means of transferring property to the husband, and this fact forms the background to Lord Hardwicke's Act reforming the conduct of marriage in 1753. Some of its rigidity, which remains in the present legislation, was brought about by the fears of the propertied classes in that generation about secret marriages. It seems anomalous that their fears should still govern our marriage laws. Cohabitation now (as then) gives no automatic rights to the partner's property, either during the partner's lifetime or (more significantly) after death or separation, whereas the married status does. If, however, dependence can be demonstrated, a claim may be upheld by the courts under the Inheritance (Provision for Dependents) Act. In the case of both marriage and cohabitation the preparation of a will indicating that the partner/spouse is beneficiary, or that their children are beneficiaries, does clarify that a common fund of property has been created which is to be passed on. Where such a precaution has been taken, then that couple's partnership does serve the same economic function as a marriage. Without such arrangements some of the automatic rights and protections for the parties are lacking. As I have indicated in chapter two, this can leave some survivors very poorly treated.

6. *Marriage can be a means of establishing an alliance between the wife's kin and her husband, or between the two families generally.*
   Such alliance-forming marriages are well known from European history, and some of the largest late mediaeval empires were built as much on well-schemed royal marriages as on conquest. Such diplomatic unions were found lower down the social scale, and in more recent times, too, as the memorial plaques on the walls of the church here can testify. They also are commonplaces in the anthropological literature; a researcher was once informed,

'We marry our enemies'. It was a serious explanation of the use of marriage in forming alliances and limiting violence in that culture, not a mother-in-law joke.

However, in modern Britain the use of marriage in forming family alliances is negligible, at least as a deliberate part of the institution. In practice in-laws are likely to become part of the family circle, and some interest in their doings and concern or even support for their well-being may develop, especially if the families live near each other. It is not part of the package, however, and is as likely not to occur. The same is true of cohabitation. It will mean as much as the couple and their families of birth make of it, though because of the uncertain beginning of the relationship any co-operation may take longer to develop. Other factors will play their part too, like existing friendships, old school ties, and so forth.

Another consideration is how far cohabitation is a means of avoiding ties or commitments to in-laws. A friend once remarked that so-called 'trial marriages' might actually be times of testing not the couple's compatibility, but of gauging the degree to which their respective parents could be tolerated. Given that caring for elderly parents is increasingly becoming part of a person's life cycle that is a serious possibility, though it is more likely to be a subconscious motive than a deliberate calculation.

7. *The formal marriage ceremony not only legitimizes children (section 1 above) but legitimizes and defines the relationship of the man and woman concerned to the satisfaction of their parents, wider kin, and society at large.* They know where they stand. To a certain (sometimes limited) extent it grants identity and moral responsibility to the couple independent of their families of birth.

When people write or talk about the wedding as being 'the bride's big day,' they are recognizing this. When a father says as the couple drive away, 'Well, she's on her own now' (meaning that he no longer feels directly responsible for his daughter now that he has given her away) he is recognizing that a transition has taken place. She has moved from one degree of respectability to another. Perhaps she has left one rather drab existence at home with mum to another equally drab state in her own home, but at least she has done so with the family's support in a grand day of glory and status. The functions of the wedding ceremonies are further discussed below.

An eighth characteristic, which appears in the Christian understanding of marriage but is omitted in this sociological list despite its social dimension, is affection – the mutual support and comfort given on an emotional level as well as on the level of economics or respectability. While marriage is an important source of this support, it cannot effectively be its only *locus*. In the past many social and emotional supports came from other sources – the extended family, or the lifelong relationships which develop in a small and relatively stable community. We do marriages a disservice if we expect them to bear all the burdens which friendship, kinship and neighbourliness once bore. Yet because of the mobility of our society, as people are moved in connection with their work, or choose to move to more pleasant or prestigious surroundings, the married partnership may be the only stable factor in a couple's circle of regular social contacts. This can place a strain upon it. Conversely, we do friendship and neighbourliness a disservice if we read a Freudian dimension into every relationship. Without being naïve we can accept that individuals may quite properly meet their needs for educational and cultural self-expression, deep friendship and soul-baring outside of marriage.

The functions of cohabitation

We now compare cohabitation with these functions of

marriage. Do they indicate that a *de facto* marriage exists?[3]

The explicitly Christian characteristics of marriage were consent and covenant, mutual support, the procreation of children and the right enjoyment of sexual instincts, with lifelong intent. A cohabiting couple will probably not have expressed their covenant with each other formally (though a few may draw up a form of contract with one another), but equally their relationship is based on a mutual consent, and will offer as much or as little emotional support as a conventional marriage. Despite the lack of a formal cohabitation contract, they may nevertheless have jointly undertaken certain major contractual commitments. They will lack the moral support given by the institution of marriage itself – the feeling that you are part of something which is bigger than you which can support you through difficult times in your relationship when the temptation to give up on it would be strong if it was just a private arrangement. They also lack the moral and social hedge (such as it is) around a marriage expressed in the phrase 'let no man put asunder'.

Legal constraints may hinder some of the financial support which is found in or after conventional marriage. The legal position of the cohabitant father is tenuous; in practice the family life need not differ from that in a conventional marriage. Sexual fidelity within the relationship need be no less than with a married couple. Some critics will doubt whether sexual expression is right within the relationship at all. If the relationship amounts to a marriage, then surely it is right. Lifelong intent will be harder to assess, but that is now sadly true of marriage. Am I the only clergyman who has had to discourage a bride from joking about divorce as she signs the marriage registers?

We next compare cohabitation with the list of sociological characteristics of marriage. The first was the legitimation of children. Clearly cohabitation does not do this. However, the current development of English law is to minimize the significance of illegitimate birth. The Family Law Reform Act of 1987 is the most recent step in this direction, implying (for instance) that unless explicitly excluded an illegitimate child is included in the general provisions of a will. But he still does not have the right to apply for probate if his parents die, nor does his father automatically become his sole guardian if his mother dies, as would be the case if his parents were married. I believe the law is unfair here in assuming that unmarried parents will not be living together and still requiring a responsible cohabiting father to go to the courts before he can exercise parental rights. The couple are able, however, through such recourse to the courts and the careful preparation of their wills, to remove from their children most of the disabilities of illegitimacy.

No 'marital rights' in law are conferred by cohabitation, and the parties remain their own masters in this respect. Informally, however, the couple have an obvious interest in each other's sexual activity. Infidelity is likely to produce the same outrage as it would if the couple were married.

Control of income and capital (items, 3, 4 & 5 in the above list) is governed by a whole complex of tax, inheritance and benefit law. Hitherto there has been no overall policy in Britain, and some provisions have benefited the cohabiting couple – the most obvious being double mortgage relief – while others have favoured the married. The Finance Bill 1988 and associated proposals ironed out many of these anomalies, and showed an explicit policy bias towards marriage by initiating a 'married couple's allowance'. However, in making the wife responsible for her own tax affairs, so bowing to feminist criticism, the Chancellor made marriage less relevant in the management of 'economic services' between a couple so that marriage is becoming more like cohabitation in this respect.

In pensions and other benefits, both national and private, the situation favours a married couple, unless in a private scheme cohabitants have been careful in their choice of policy and in nominating each other as beneficiaries. A wife benefits from her husband's National Insurance contributions, but a cohabitant does not, and may lose DSS benefit because her man is deemed to be supporting her. (He may claim extra for her as his 'house-keeper' if she will let him.) This seems anomalous and possibly immoral quite apart from the unpleasantness of snooping and possible blackmail. She is contributing to the domestic economy of the household in the same way as a wife, yet cannot reap the benefits of her man's contributions. But because she is part of that domestic economy she is debarred from making claims in her own right. As a result some potentially stable relationships, which might move towards marriage, are weakened.

In the event of an intestate death cohabitation does not establish a common fund of property which will pass automatically to the survivor, or is available to maintain their children. Case-law has however looked favourably recently on survivors who have been dependent on the deceased or his property, and affiliation orders can be used to obtain maintenance from an estate. Similarly if a cohabitation breaks up, case law has been increasingly inclined to support a claim to beneficial interest in (say) a shared home when it can be argued that it was intended to involve the same degree of commitment as a marriage.[4]

In the points covered in the last three paragraphs the distinction between marriage and cohabitation is still there, but is either ambiguous or growing less significant. If, however, a couple choose positively to remain as unmarried partners in order to keep the law out of their private world they are making a miscalculation, for they will need more help from the lawyers in drawing up a will, or if tragedy looms. But wish such help cohabitation serves many of the economic functions of marriage; without that extra effort some of the rights and protection inherent for the parties in marriage are lacking.

Cohabitation serves the purpose of establishing an 'alliance' only in so far as the parties to it, and their families, wish it to, but in English society at present that is also true of marriage. In relation to item 6 on the list, the two states signify the same in modern Britain.

In conclusion, the absence of a formal marriage does make a difference to the couple who cohabit. But it will, if the worst comes, attract some of the legal protections inherent in marriage, and legal arrangements can be made to give it more of them. If such arrangements are made, the relationship can show sufficient of the functional characteristics of marriage to be given the moral dignity of marriage.

If this is granted, then the question must arise as to when a cohabitation become a 'quasi-marriage'. Lawyers have found difficulty (at least in England) in answering this. The DSS has found less difficulty, but they are dealing with weekly payments so they ask whether a person is being supported during a specific period. Social scientists have used definitions such as four or five nights spent together per week over a three- or six-month period. Other jurisdictions have chosen a longer period (from six months to four years) or the birth of a child as a criterion.

In moral terms, I suggest, if the couple decide to draw up a specific contract then they should be given the respect of husband and wife. Where they do not (and very few do) I suggest that cohabitation becomes quasi-marital when some major joint commitment is made, in line with points 3 & 4 above. If they are living together this might be the joint registration of their child, or the opening of a joint bank account, joint purchase of a house where they are to live, or perhaps joint rental of it, or even the signing of mutual wills (i.e., in line with point 5). These ideas reflect the functions of marriage discussed above. Some of them already attract legal consequences as if the couple were married (especially if they are engaged). If there are obligations to an existing or previous spouse the picture becomes more complex. I deal with that in another chapter, but such obligations cannot be ignored.

The functions of the day – a family affair

Just as the state of matrimony functions in other ways than those expressed in the Christian wedding service, the same is true of the ceremony and attendant celebration itself. These other functions will vary with the circumstances. Some of these functions are highlighted by popular writing or comments on the subject.

The wedding ceremony is not simply the legal business in the register office or the church service. It includes the various receptions and parties. It can become a demonstration by the couple or their families of status and achievements. Thus a couple who only want a simple affair with a few of their friends find that their day is taken over by the family. Or they themselves will defer the actual ceremony until they can afford the reception and disco which they feel bound to provide, even though they already live together. Or the family will refuse a quick wedding, even though the couple are already living together, so that they can save up to give their daughter a big send-off. Just as in the morality-conscious nineteenth century a proper wedding conferred 'respectability',[5] so now the conspicuous consumption at some weddings demonstrates that the family or the couple has made it in a society dominated by economic values. Conversely, just as it was argued in connection with Lord Hardwicke's Act that the legal regulation of marriage, with its attendant cost, would deter couples from marriage, so now the cost of the receptions can do the same.

This may seem cynical, but it does represent some of the reasons why thinking couples avoid a wedding. I feel a great deal of sympathy for a couple who resent *their* day being taken over by the rest of the family (who may subconsciously be staging the wedding which they wanted twenty-five years before). Such resentment is understandable in a generation which thinks very much in individualistic terms. But for all that, we are not entirely individuals, and a wedding is not the bride's or the couple's day alone.

It is a day for the families. It is often said as the reception breaks up that it is only at weddings and funerals that a scattered family gets together. The family has an interest in such celebrations. To deny the opportunity for such an expression of unity can cause offence and hurt. The impropriety felt by the older relatives of a couple who cohabit may include an element of sadness that no such gathering is to take place, as well as unease about the morality of their sexual relationship.

As a family day it is also an opportunity for those who have been concerned with the couple in their growth to express formally their concern and goodwill, and to give them a proper sendoff in a new and more independent stage in their lives. They may or may not be particular friends of the couple, but they have been part of the network of support that has helped the couple or their parents in their formative years. Their invitation to the wedding is a public acknowledgement and a thankful recognition of that; lack of a wedding can leave a feeling of anticlimax. The liner has drifted from its moorings, not been launched with champagne. Here is a latent social function which is often overlooked.

The concern and goodwill expressed at a wedding may not only be for the couple, but also for their immediate families. A widowed mother has told me of the support and sympathy she felt from the guests at the wedding of her last child. Not only were they recognizing that she would now be alone, but they were also congratulating her by their presence on bringing up her family single-handed.

If I am right in seeing such latent family and community business being transacted under the cover of the wedding, and if it is right that such gratitude and support within the couple's network should be expressed, then this represents a strong argument for a formal wedding of some kind. The couple are not isolated individuals, and for them to act as if they were and turn their relationship into a private arrangement (however committed and sincere), is a vote of no confidence in that network. Perhaps that is a vote which they do wish to pass. They have not felt the support of the network, or have even felt ensnared by it. Or perhaps they foresee too clearly the conspicuous consumption which will be easier to sidestep by cohabitation than to resist in planning a wedding. Thus I would argue strongly for the public ceremonies because of their latent social importance as well as their patent legal value. But I would respect a decision not to go public if it is made advisedly, responsibly and after serious thought. I would want to suggest to such a couple, however, that the ceremony is also an opportunity for them to celebrate each other; it is a public declaration of the value in which they hold each other and their relationship.

The difference in being married

So does marriage make a difference, especially if a couple have already been living together for some time? Or is stable cohabitation de facto a second (or perhaps third) variation on the forms of marriage which British custom, if not English law, recognizes at the end of the twentieth century – alongside those begun with a church wedding or a register office ceremony? That can be answered on three levels. In legal terms there is a difference, for marriage is the most straightforward way of arranging a package of benefits which would otherwise have to be sorted out piecemeal, and in most cases are not.

There is also the emotional level, which has not so far been touched on in detail. Those couples to whom I have spoken about their planned weddings after some time of cohabitation do not expect that it will make a difference. What matters, after all, is their feeling for each other – isn't it? It is not as easy as that. I have already mentioned the feeling of being caught up in a structure that is bigger than you are, which lends its support when times are hard. That is an awareness that some people will feel, either as a positive factor or in a negative way – 'I can't let everybody down, I can't break my word.' Even that negative factor may be something which will work constructively to preserve a relationship while problems are sorted out. Perhaps, for those who can think in such terms, that is how sacramental grace in marriage may operate. The absence of such a structure may work the other way. Without the bond of marriage, cohabitant individuals may feel a nagging fear that their partner will not stay, and will not be there when they return, especially if the lifestyle of either partner involves a lot of time away from the shared home. For others still it may be the fact of marriage which produces the problems – so that one or other feels trapped by it, whereas previously there was a freedom in their mutual self-giving that is lost. There are instances of long cohabitation followed by a marriage ending soon afterwards in divorce for this reason. Others have looked back on their weddings and said that it does make a positive difference. They would not have felt right if their relationship had not led into marriage, even though they were not unhappy about it before. It did lead to a sense of greater security and belonging. Perhaps all that can be said is that on an emotional, empirical level, the difference will be there, but that each couple (and perhaps each individual) will experience that difference differently, because of the varied expectations and emotional baggage that they bring with them to the altar.

The third answer to the question whether cohabitation is *de facto* a modern British variant of marriage, is yes – in many cases but not all. On the anthropological level, despite the legal differences between formal marriage and cohabitation, I suggest that there can be enough overlapping features from those on Leach's list for us to regard it in that light.

Recognition of marriage

The conclusion reached at the end of the previous section leads on to still more questions. Our society copes with two institutions, marriage and cohabitation. It acknowledges marriages as its legitimate offspring. The position of cohabitation is less clear; some would disown it. An obvious moral question for many Christians is how can they accept a pattern of behaviour which appears to be a form of extra-marital relationship, and lacks any formal basis in law?

My main argument, that society has institutionalized cohabitation even if the law has not yet caught up with social practice, answers that question in one way. It implies that a stable cohabitation is as legitimate as marriage because social custom, whether codified in the law or not, is what defines marriage. If that is so, stable cohabitation is not extra-marital. Those who disagree with this premise may disprove it in a number of ways. They may either argue factually that cohabiting relationships are not sufficiently institutionalized to be treated in that way, or argue ethically that custom is irrelevant because it is the law of the state alone which defines marriage,[6] or pragmatically that the state can only tolerate one such institution.[7]

Alternatively, they might accept that in secular terms stable cohabitation is a form of marriage, but argue that it lacks so many of those qualities which mark out a Christian marriage that it does not merit Christian recognition. With this alternative there is a catch. If cohabitation is acceptable in secular terms but not in Christian terms, what is it that makes legal marriage acceptable in Christian terms? Is it its qualities as marriage, or the state's dictät? In that last case we are moving out of the realm of sexual ethics into political theory.

We saw that the view that the state alone has authority to define marriage was that imposed on England by Lord Hardwicke's Act. Since it was the Church of England that was to operate his system it appeared that what was being imposed was a 'Christian' view of marriage. At that time that was close enough to the truth, since divorce was then impossible except by private Act of Parliament and the church's vows of loyalty and permanence 'before God and this congregation' were the ones used by the state. The church has retained that privileged role, despite the addition of civil registrars in 1837. It is therefore all too easy for Anglicans and those with a similar viewpoint to identify marriage according to English law with Christian marriage and so to assume that 'the inauguration of marriage takes place by whatever means is currently recognized in a particular nation.'[8] Such trust in the law of the land is misplaced. A particular state may countenance forms of marriage, or a doctrine of marriage which are very distant from the Christian ideal.

It is a moot point whether marriage in England today falls

under that criticism. The affirmation signed by a couple giving notice to a registrar of their intention to marry speaks of their exclusive, lifelong, voluntary union,[9] and the declarations in a church service state the same. However, because of the way in which various divorce laws have progressively altered the practice of marriage since the mid-nineteenth century it could be argued that the doctrine of marriage espoused by this state denies the Christian ideal. It is now possible to petition for divorce after one year, and to obtain divorce by consent after two, though the courts have to oversee that process. Is this 'union . . . for life'? Whatever results from current (1993/4) proposals for the reform of divorce procedures, this criticism is going to remain.

Whatever one's appraisal of the institution of marriage in England, examples can be cited from other jurisdictions in which the state recognizes marriages which are far from the Christian ideal. Thus Alfred Guillaume describes the practice of *mut'a* marriages in Shi'a Muslim countries,[10] which were contracted for a fee and might by prior agreement last for only a few days while a traveller was in the place where his wife lived. The state cannot be a Christian's final arbiter over the beginning or validity of marriage, even if its requirements will be taken seriously.

There is a catch in this. If the state is not in itself competent to define marriage, then society's custom and practice are hardly more competent. Society may give birth to new institutions, which is what I take to be happening with cohabitation at present. It may modify and adapt existing ones, deliberately or incidentally, as has happened with formal marriage down the years. It may take hold of the new and consciously shape them, as I suggest should be done with cohabitation. But in each of these cases a moral appraisal goes on, even if people's pattern of thinking is so identified with what they see around them that appraisal is simply approval. I suggest that Christians can appraise both current law, and custom and practice, in the areas of marriage and cohabitation in the light of the Christian ideals discussed in chapter 4 and 5, and also with reference to the sociological criteria in this chapter. From the sociology I have argued that stable cohabitation should be treated socially as a form of marriage alongside the marriage conceived legally in a church or register office. From the Christian ideals I believe all forms of marriage in Britain, or in any other State, can be assessed morally and all will to a greater or lesser extent be found wanting.[11] The same may be said of each individual relationship, whether cohabitant or ratified by marriage in church or before a registrar.

The fact that they are found wanting does not prevent us from treating them with the dignity of marriage, feeling hurt in so far as they fall short, and in prayer, counselling or social action seeking (as appropriate) to improve them. There is a scene, I think in C.S. Lewis's science fiction novel, *Out of the Silent Planet*, in which the semi-divine rulers of Mars bow to Professor Ransom, the central character, because in his humanity he bears the image of God. Fallen being that he is he rejects the homage, knowing his own moral and physical frailty and unworthiness, but is told to accept it graciously, because of the image that he still bears. Despite the frailty and unworthiness of human relationships there is something in them which can still reflect the mystery of God's love for us. I believe we can still bow, even while we look for deeper love and maybe try to engineer greater commitment through the law.

When the early church began its struggle to teach the pagan world the qualities of Christian marriage there were those who wanted to write off relationships which did not concur with the legal requirements. Thus we see Hippolytus reluctantly telling slave girls to remain exclusively loyal to the men who had taken them as concubines, and required Christian men who took women in this way to treat the relationship as marriage. He would rather the unmarried 'be steadfast' or marry *kata nomon* – according to customary law – which in Rome discouraged unions between slave and free. But by telling a man to treat his slave concubine as a Christian *wife* he is challenging the customary law to a limited extent. But he did not let himself carry that to the logical conclusion that Pope Callistus did. The Pope wished to treat the relationship of a free woman and a slave man as Christian marriage, while Hippolytus saw such a liaison beneath her station as a reason for excommunicating the woman unless she put away the man. The case is, of course, not entirely parallel with modern cohabitation, which is a freely entered relationship, not forced by the institution of slavery. I still think Callistus' principle can be applied; the less than legal liaison should be respected, strengthened and brought nearer the Christian ideal.

Notes

1. Cf. E.K. Gough 'The Nayars and the Definition of Marriage', *J.R.A.I. vol.89* p.23ff and E.R. Leach, 'Polyandry, Inheritance and the Definition of Marriage', *Man, Vol.54* (1955) p.182ff. These articles are effectively the conclusion of a long debate among social anthropologists. The list which follows is a shortened version of theirs, which I first printed in *Marriage before Marriage?* Grove Brooks, Nottingham, 1988 p.18.
2. In *Taking It Like a Woman*, cited in Liz Hodgkinson, *Unholy Matrimony*.
3. This section and the following one represent a slight revision of what I wrote originally in *Marriage before Marriage?*
4. E.g. Griffiths L.J. in Bernard v. Josephs (2 *WLR* 1052 at p.1061), cited by Barton, *op. cit.* chap. 1.
5. Suggested in *An Honourable Estate* (C.I.O. London, 1988), Sections 70 & 67.
6. cf. E. Pratt, *Living in Sin?* p.5.
7. Tim Stafford, in *Sexual Chaos*, IVP, Leicester 1993 (Illinois 1989) p.117f. argues (in an American context) against cohabitation on the grounds that today's communities are too weak and populations are too unstable and walking away too easy for us to recognize private promises without public ratification. It is also true that today's communities have chosen not to try to enforce private promises; breach of promise suits were removed from Common Law in England in 1970.
8. Pratt, p.5. He thus makes himself a slave to fortune; if

Parliament should decree that on the 14th Feb. next all couples who have lived together for more than a year are married, will he accept that with no moral qualms?

9. In line with the definition in Hyde v. Hyde in 1866.
10. *Islam*, Penguin, Harmondsworth 1956 p.103f. Tim Severin in *The Sindbad Voyage,* Hutchinson, London 1982, pp.128ff. describes the working of this custom among Omanis visiting Calicut.
11. This is examined by Gary Jenkins in his study *Cohabitation; a Biblical Perspective*, Grove, Nottingham 1992, especially pp.10-19.

SIX

Cohabitation

Before going into details about the reasons why people cohabit, and the problems this may entail for them, I wish to state again that I am not concerned here with discussing or defending casual affairs or promiscuous behaviour. Though the word 'cohabitation' is sometimes used as a euphemism for such activity, that is not how I am using it, nor do I intend what I say about cohabitation to be used to justify promiscuity. The word comes, of course, from Latin roots meaning *to reside with*, and now has the connotation of residence together *as if husband and wife*.

What cohabitation is not

There are those who live under the same roof, but for whom that arrangement is simply a matter of sharing common residence. There may well be friendship – it would be difficult to maintain such an arrangement without a degree of friendliness – but no quasi-marital relationship is intended. The rather cumbersome phrase '*living apart together*' has been coined for such an arrangement, sometimes shortened to L.A.T. I say this, because it is easy to jump to the wrong conclusions, and so cause offence or embarrassment to people living in this way. They may themselves use the phrase 'I'm living with so and so' incautiously, giving rise to blushes or merriment, depending on the context. We may smile, but especially if we wish to adopt a critical attitude to cohabitation we need to be sensitive to the actual circumstances of such people, and not jump to wrong conclusions. Nevertheless, some of the points made below about clarifying ownership and responsibilities, and about awareness of the potential financial losses involved in such an arrangement, will apply to 'L.A.T.' couples and groups as much as cohabitants.

This would also be true of any form of shared occupation of a home, by adult sons or daughters and a parent, or by brothers and sisters, or by a homosexual couple. I do not intend to go into such relationships here, but some discussion with a lawyer would be advisable for anyone in such a situation.

In particular, I am aware that some of my arguments might be used to validate homosexual 'marriage,' by the back door so to speak. That is not my intention, and I believe a whole range of other ethical issues come into play in this particular case. Just as in English law, marriage is defined in terms of a union between *one man and one woman*, so in this discussion of cohabitation I am concerned only with heterosexual unions and do not wish to get into those other issues.

If one confusion is to equate cohabitation with promiscuity, another is to think of it just as a teenage issue. This is not a discussion about 'teenage sex', or even just about couples in their twenties. While the peak years at the moment for cohabitation are people's twenties and early thirties, some of the cohabitant couples I have known have been in their fifties and sixties and beyond. Some of the most poignant stories of the problems which are thrown up by cohabitation relate to older couples. This is hardly surprising, since questions of bereavement, inheritance and pension entitlements are less likely to arise earlier. I recently took the funeral of a man in his sixties whose first wife had died, and who lived for ten years or so with another woman. They had spoken of marriage, but never got round to it – except for promises made to each other in private before God in a chapel in France. Were they married? I did not think it right in the circumstances to probe as to why they had not formally married, despite talking about it. I suspect that for some older people there is an embarrassment about the romantic razmatazz that goes with a wedding in the popular mind. All that, they feel, is for the young, not for them. Hence they put off what could be a very quiet and relatively private matter.

Yet another confusion in this debate is the question of single parenthood, and the very real social problems that arise for the single parent, and for her or his children. Cohabiting parents are not single, though quirks in the way statistics are recorded or in the way a relationship is hidden from the DSS may make them appear so. Cohabiting parents may be more likely to split than married parents, so this point is not totally irrelevant, but stable cohabitants should hardly be blamed for the failures of those who separate, any more than married couples should be berated for the divorce rate. The real issue, in the case of cohabitants and married couples alike, is how to encourage wholesome stability.

What cohabitation is

A definition of cohabitation is difficult. What suits a sociologist may not be precise enough for a lawyer, and different definitions will throw up different statistics perhaps with different moral implications. Of the fifty-six per cent of couples who live together before formal marriage how many have consciously chose cohabitation initially as an alternative lifestyle to marriage, and how many chose to move in together once their marital home had been purchased, but after the marriage plans had been made? At one end of the spectrum a sociologist may study as cohabitants those who spend four or five nights together during a week over a three month period. At the other end, South Australian lawyers recognize four years of joint residence, or the birth of a child, as giving rights of inheritance if one of the partners dies intestate. They also accept a form of Declarator similar to their Scottish colleagues. Scots lawyers now, apparently, expect a three-year period to have been spent together, though in time past another provision – the registration of irregular marriages – enabled far speedier unions to be ratified. During the First World War an English bishop (Lincoln, I believe) complained that single women in his diocese whose children had been fathered by now dead soldiers could claim no widow's support, whereas Scots women in the same situation were treated as married.

If it is ever right to regard cohabitation as equivalent to marriage, I believe that it is to the longer end of this spectrum that we should look before we give it that status, and that other criteria as well should be applied to assess how closely a particular relationship comes to conventional marriage, and what the couple's intentions are in respect of legal marriage. These criteria will correspond to the social functions noted as part of the married relationship in the previous chapter. How open and public is the relationship at least among their peers or is it a secret 'affair'? Are both parties parenting any children there may be? Is it a sexually exclusive relationship? Is there a degree of co-operation over present and future finances and domestic arrangements? Have the couple left their homes of birth to cleave to each other and offer emotional support? The couple will also have to meet some assessable legal criteria, and in chapter 8 I shall attempt to suggest what those might be.

Reasons for cohabiting

So why do people cohabit? The motives are mixed, and manifold. The obvious opportunity for sexual love is part of it as Ted Pratt suggests[1], but for a number of reasons I believe we should not assume that it is the only, or even the main reason. Cohabitation may combine, in Oscar Wilde's phrase about marriage, maximum temptation with maximum opportunity, and add to that a hint of forbidden fruit. Temptation, opportunity and inclination are however by no means restricted to those who live together. For some, cohabitation may indeed begin with a casual night together, which becomes a weekend, and then extends. For others their partnership may have grown from friendship through a sexual relationship to the conscious decision to move in together. No doubt they do not feel the need to keep their sexual liaison furtive, but more significantly they do want partnership.

Sexuality is an important and powerful motivating force in our lives, but we should recognize that there are others. It is wrong for Christians to sell the pass completely to a (so-called) Freudian view of human personality, still less to surrender to prurience in our own thinking. If a couple say that they decided to buy a flat and move in together in advance of their marriage because the flat became available in a place they wanted at a price they could manage, then we should give them credit for knowing their own minds and making their own decisions. That may seem naïve when so much in the modern media tells us that sex is paramount, but it is a temptation that we should resist. To do otherwise will actually undermine all morality, rather than uphold Christian morals, since it reduces moral choice to biological function.

Financial considerations in some cases explain why couples cohabit before or instead of marrying. The example just quoted of the availability of a flat is one instance of this. Payment for accommodation is said to take up as much as a third of a person's disposable income. If so, it does make sense for a couple with no rooted objection to it and who do not or will not live with their parents to live together in anticipation of marriage rather than pay rent on two flats. The couple who gave me that explanation of their actions wanted to live in a particular much sought after district, and at the time prices were rising fast. Perhaps they were morally wrong. Perhaps their decision was overhasty and unwise practically. As it turned out the church wedding was cancelled. I am not sure whether they went in the end to the register office, though their intention to marry was one of the factors in their decision to live together. Perhaps sexual attractions weighed heavier than they knew. Nevertheless, the motive they were conscious of was linked with finance.

The other financial consideration is the cost of the wedding itself. I cannot be the only clergyman who has been told by the parents of the child they want baptised, 'We're going to get married when we can afford it.' They may even go as far as another couple whom I know, who booked the date, only to ring up some months later to cancel it. The father, self-employed in the building trade, had received an unexpected and large tax demand, which absorbed the money set aside for the wedding.

It is not the church fees (or the registrar's fees for that matter) which present the problem. At the time of writing they hardly add up to £100. It is all the paraphernalia that go along with the ceremony that incur the real cost. I recently took a wedding which cost, I was told, £10,000. That is not in a particularly affluent parish. Four figure sums are the norm, for events which begin with the hire of suits, the hairdressing, and progress via the church and the photographs to a family reception followed by a disco for friends and work colleagues. Faced with the peer pressure to provide such a do at such a cost it is small wonder that many couples defer 'The Day'. Small wonder also if their parents indicate that they will have to find much of the cost themselves.

There is another side to this; we should not dismiss such conspicuous consumption out of hand. For some there is the wish to have a splendid celebration, and to enjoy it. It is an expression of their success and generosity as well as of how much they value each other. There are also obligations to match the generosity of others to whose weddings they have been invited in the past, and perhaps a desire at least to match their show. The parents as well as the couple may be motivated, consciously or subconsciously, in such a way.

For others such a grand event is just too daunting. It is not that they do not wish to spend so much, nor that they do not yet have it to spend, but they know they would be overwhelmed. In this they share the motives of many of those in the 18th century who sought clandestine, and (after 1753) licensed weddings. Their way of overcoming the social expectations that go with the wedding day is to sidestep it altogether. This may especially be so if they sense it will be taken over by the family and be an opportunity for them to put on their show. Writers such as J.R. Gillis have noted how as the effects of the Hardwicke Act took effect the social élite sought to avoid grand public weddings in which their village communities would be involved, while those who wished to be part of the élite used elaborate weddings as a means of asserting their claims.[2]

I have a great deal of sympathy with couples who want to play down the ostentation of their wedding, and who want theirs to be a simple celebration. I can see why some want to avoid it altogether. I do, however, believe that there is value in celebration. It is a way of expressing the worth they see in each other, and their appreciation of what their families have done for them in their upbringing. I do not believe celebration requires extravagance.

But there is another side to this coin too. Where the family has not seemed of much help, and there is no wish to involve them in what is seen as a private affair between the couple, many of the social reasons for marriage disappear (thought not all, as I shall show later) and cohabitation seems the right course.

Some couples are unable to contract a legal marriage.[3] This is the case of those who are legally bound by an existing marriage, and have not obtained a divorce. I deal with the separate issue of divorce and remarriage in chapter 7. Such a couple may intend to seek marriage once a divorce is obtained. Others may not want marriage and may not even want the divorce, especially if rights to maintenance or pension are involved. (This may seem morally questionable – wanting the best of both worlds – but such motivation could be morally laudable, if for instance a man did not wish to deprive his separated wife of her pension rights in his name. Not every case is identical.)

Marriage itself may seem an emotional threat to some in this situation. Their previous experience has battered them so much that they fear its repetition or doubt their own ability to give what marriage promises. While they want and probably need the support of a loving partner, they fear, consciously or subconsciously, that tying the knot will leave them bound in chains again.

I know of other couples and individuals for whom that emotional reaction is linked with a fear that for them it is marriage itself which is jinxed. The tragic end of a happy marriage, rather than the welcome end of a tragic marriage, is what makes them hesitant over a new commitment which may also be cut short. Such reasons may seem irrational, but they should not be dismissed insensitively.

Most frequently blamed for the rise in cohabitation is the experience of parents' unhappy marriages or bitter divorces. If that is what marriage is, think the couple, then we want a better relationship untrammelled by all the social baggage that marriage brings with it. If that is how a marriage ends, we don't want to risk ending up feeling that angrily about each other. The sad thing about both these reactions is that cohabitation can turn out just as unhappy, and lead to just as complicated and bitter a disentanglement as formal marriage. But again, irrational though they may seem, they are often heartfelt and should be respected.

One of the points made about marriage in the Church of England services is that it should not be undertaken lightly and unadvisedly. How are we to react to a couple who have thought seriously about formal marriage, and then rejected it? Their reasons may be varied, and conscientious. What of the couple I described earlier who looked at the high demands of the marriage vows, and felt unable, or even unworthy, to attain them? They loved each other, and wanted to support each other, but doubted their strength to live up to what we offer them in the Christian ideals of marriage and so opt for the lesser commitment of cohabitation. The sad irony is that their honesty held them back from a relationship which many others enter with little forethought and less candour.

I was told about this couple second-hand, so could not contribute to their thinking myself. I would want to say to them that the Christian promise in marriage is not just a list of high demands or inspiring concepts such as sacrament or covenant, but a promise of grace; that is to say, a promise that we can draw on God's moral and emotional resources to support us when our own are lacking; that he does not expect us to be the perfect husband or wife, reflecting his character at every move, but that he gives his forgiveness and the power to forgive and be forgiven when we are not perfect. In short, he gives his Holy Spirit, who is as much at home when invited in family life as at a prayer meeting.

Is marriage a defective institution?

Or what are we to say to the couples – or perhaps the women – who have looked at marriage as we practise it and have practised it down the years, and see in our institution of marriage something which downgrades women, treating them as adjuncts to their male partner?[4] They have a case, though a declining one. Until the Married Women's Property Act husbands owned their wives' property; only as recently as 1988 tax law was changed to make separate declaration by wife and husband the norm; even now the married allowance is credited by the Inland Revenue to the husband's account unless it is explicitly transferred. In 1909 a woman writer could term marriage the only trade that most women had been trained in. Such examples may seem trivial, but they highlight a feature of society which many people, now taught increasingly to value themselves as individuals, resent and reject. Hodgkinson criticizes the dependency of women, and even the idea of interdependence as psychologically demeaning.[5] They love each other and wish to be committed to each other, but not in *that* way. We may disagree with them, but the point has to be argued. It is they who have to live with the institution they are uneasy in, even if we are happy with it.

For the couple who have thought through their relationship in this way I have respect. I would expect them to have made alternative arrangements as a sign of their commitment, using mutual wills, joint property agreements, and such like. Some actually come to formal 'cohabitation contracts', but the legal validity of these is in doubt. The law is held to frown on anything which might undermine the institution of marriage, or inhibit a person's rights to marry freely; a contract which links sexual and financial relationship is held to be immoral and therefore unenforceable. But none of these points has been tested in case-law in modern times, so a well prepared contract might be valid. Anyone thinking along theses lines would do well to see a lawyer. I believe the English law should be clarified to allow such contracts, and that they should be treated as a form of civil marriage, as I shall explain later. I might well agree with some of the criticisms such people level at the way marriage works in Britain as an institution, though my inclination would be to reform the institution rather than urge people to opt out of it, and to live within it in such a way that the criticisms were made invalid.

In answer to their main point, however, I would make two responses. The institution of marriage may historically have treated women as inferior and even exploited them: they could not handle their own financial affairs; they were tied to the kitchen sink, and so on. However, it has also offered protection and a redress against other forms of exploitation; they could not be casually dismissed or thrown out, even if their rights were limited. Marriage is a remedy against the sins of *unrestrained* male dominance, even where it does allow some of the ills of dominance. And that is the second response; without some structure and some restraint the new morality, with its stress on individual values and choices, easily becomes a cloak for the old immorality, in which it is more likely the woman who will be let down.

And what is to be said to those who argue that personal relationships are not the proper business of the law? They see no reason to allow the state into their bedrooms and so object in principle to the legal niceties of a marriage, even though they confess themselves to be committed to each other and might claim that the legalities would actually demean their love. Once again the new morality can hide what turns out in the end to be the old exploitation. When things are going well for a couple they do not need the law, but it comes into its own when trouble comes. That is not necessarily the breakdown of their love, but personal tragedy or death. Marriage governs a great deal of what goes on in our human relationships in addition to our sex lives.

A trial for marriage?

The list is a long one, and many more variations could be added to it. I shall, however, end it with the idea of trial marriage; a couple are not sure whether they are right for each other, and want to see how they get on together before actually making a permanent commitment. There is something admirable in this; the couple are prepared to think and work at their relationship before making more definite commitments. However, the logician in me doubts whether you can test out a relationship which is intended to be permanent and binding by engaging in one which is by definition tentative and not binding. Perhaps one of the reasons why those who have cohabited are more likely to split than those who have not is that they expected marriage to be just like things were before, when in fact they are not. Emotionally and legally, socially and personally there are differences which may not be easy to pinpoint, but which subtly change the relationship. For some, in fact, the anxiety – *will he still be there when I get home?* – is removed. For others a different stress comes in – *she's got me trapped now, and I can't get away* – which undermines what seemed a good relationship. (That may be true of any cohabitant relationship which moves towards formal marriage.) A so-called 'trial marriage' may work as a relationship, but is not necessarily a trial for marriage for that couple.

Types of cohabitation

In some of the earliest studies of cohabitation, Barton[6] and Dyer and Berlins[7], list these reasons for cohabitation under five heads, which I reproduce as a summary here:

1. 'Married' – i.e. they will go through a formal ceremony when they are free to do so.
2. Committed – i.e. they have a durable relationship but do not want marriage for themselves even though they have no objection to it as such for others.
3. Exploratory – a trial, which may end, or be formalized in marriage.
4. Ideological – they reject the institution of marriage, or state interference in their lives. They may have some form of contractual relationship.
5. Casual – They have not thought through the reasons for their conduct. (This is Dyer and Berlins' word. It does not necessarily imply that they merely drifted into living together out of a casual liaison, though that may have been the case.)

This list was compiled in the early eighties when the percentage of people living together in the months leading up to their marriage was far lower than it is now. I suggest that a variation 1a should be included in the list – those who are engaged and are anticipating the formal ceremony. Those who have deferred formal marriage for financial reasons should belong in the same sub-heading (or possibly in section 2), even if there has been no engagement and no date is booked. When Karen Dunnell researched into Family Formation in 1976 she noted that only one per cent of those marrying between 1956 and 1960 had lived together before their marriage, but nine per cent of those marrying between 1970 and 1975. For most of these the length of cohabitation had been less than a year but there was a hint that the length of cohabitation before marriage was lengthening, though the number of such people in her sample was too small to show a statistically acceptable trend.[8] By 1992 other studies showed fifty-six per cent cohabiting before their marriage.

If a far less statistically sound survey of couples marrying in this parish between 1986 and 1993 is anything to go by, the length of cohabitation is now greater before the actual marriage – of a sample of 150, 32 cohabited, but only nine had been together less than a year. A few moved in together at the address given only after they had booked the wedding, but for a higher number the decision to book the wedding did not come until a few months after the move to the given address.

In discussing these reasons Barton noted that there was little information available about what couples expect out of a cohabitant relationship, and whether that expectation is the same for both partners. Dunnell's research concentrated on a sample of women partly because the analysis of different responses from partners would have proved too complex. That is still a fair comment, after nearly ten years. I believe that companionship is as important an expectation as sexual enjoyment. Security also will be a hope, though whether it is a delusion only becomes clear with time. Are women, as Pratt observes, trading sex for security and finding it a bad bargain in the long term?[9] Many relationships will seem to the couple (or to one of them) to be 'for keeps', while their families and their peers will see the cracks almost from the start, and will have regarded them as little more than casual.

Barton, as a lawyer, saw this uncertainty about people's expectation of cohabitation as a barrier to reform of the law. When some are actually trying to avoid legal interference with their relationships that is a pertinent point – but not insurmountable. Already the law is trying to say to individuals that relationships into which they entered perhaps casually and briefly have consequences and lead to responsibilities from which they cannot walk away. If we say that in connection with the support of children, it is not impossible to lay down criteria within which protection is offered to partners.

Legal differences between marriage and cohabitation

The reason why I believe there is a need for some clarification and tightening of the law is because there are pitfalls for the unwary in simple cohabitation. That is not just because the scope for deception – self-deception, or deception of one's partner – is greater. There are a number of ways in which a formal marriage serves to protect husband and wife when things go wrong which are lacking in the case of a cohabiting couple, or which are more complex. There are a number of books, long and complicated books[10], written by lawyers for other lawyers or for the lay public, which delve further into these particular issues that I can in part of a chapter now, and even they recommend a personal interview with a solicitor, rather than mere DIY law.

The legal differences between marriage and cohabitation are largely to be found in four areas:

1. tax and benefit arrangements,
2. parental rights and obligations, and inheritance,
3. the rights of the survivor on the death, especially the intestate death of one partner, and
4. property rights in the event of a split between the couple.

In the first of these, though 'public policy' is to support marriage as an institution, the fiscal system at times speaks with two voices. A couple living together cannot claim the married couple's tax allowance, but like a married couple they will now be taxed as separate individuals. If they have more than one child each can claim separately for one of the children as a 'first child' and get an extra allowance. The Community Charge (Poll Tax) treated cohabitants as jointly and severally liable for each others' payments just as if they were married couples – causing a great sense of injustice when a partner, or spouse, was deserted. If they are receiving a benefit, they will, however, be treated as a single unit, rather than separate individuals. This equates them for DSS purposes with those who are married. By cohabiting they lose benefits if they are honest about the relationship. If they are not honest they fall foul of attempts to suppress DSS fraud – a fear which may destabilize some relationships which could head towards marriage. The official guidelines do however state that the DSS must not assume a husband and wife type relationship if a couple are found at the same address. Cohabitants cannot benefit from each other's contributions toward contributory benefits such as a widow's benefit, though in some circumstances they can be included in unemployment benefit claims. Barlow comments, 'There is a tendency to treat cohabitees in the same way as spouses where this is to the advantage of the state purse, and not when it would involve extra cost.'[11] A widow loses her widow's benefit if she cohabits, but can reclaim it if she and her partner separate.

While the administration of claims based on a short-term, or a series of short-term cohabitations would probably be impracticable, I believe there is an injustice if a long-term cohabitant, who has contributed to a family's domestic economy but is denied benefits in her own right as a result, is denied the benefits of her partner's contributions, should he die. Those concerned to know precisely where they stand should consult a lawyer, Citizens' Advice Bureau or Benefits Advice Centre, or the DSS themselves. Those with higher incomes and greater capital might add an accountant to that list. I say this for the benefit of married as well as cohabitant couples; some of the advantages are weighed in their favour (by accident or design), but are of no advantage if not taken up.

In the other three areas, marriage and family law, though complex, does lay down recognized ways for the protection of the parties involved. Without marriage the law has no set procedure, may well treat a previously intimate couple as legal strangers, and often behaves in the exact opposite of what popular wisdom expects. The result is actually harsher for cohabitants than true strangers. One is likely to draw up a formal agreement with a lodger, but feel that love covers everything with a partner. Without a specific legal agreement a cohabitant has no rights to the roof over his head, even if he relinquished other property to move in, and has paid his way. The courts will assess who gave or bought or brought what, and redistribute on that clinical basis. Tenancies will not normally be transferred unless they are already in joint names. Even with shared property, unless there is a will or beneficial trust in favour of the survivor, a deceased's share may devolve on a distant relative or the Crown. The picture is complex, and these are just headlines which suggest problems likely to be encountered. The basic message is talk about it (even if it is unromantic – realism may carry the warmth of romance through the chill wind of economics) and see a lawyer.[12] That applies to any separate individuals, even within the extended family, who share accommodation on trust.

Most unmarried couples whose children I baptise expect that the registration of the child in the father's name is all that is needed to establish parentage, guardianship, and legitimacy should they later marry. They are incredulous when I suggest reregistration is necessary if they marry, or that the woman needs to specify the father as guardian in her will. Most believe that registration in the father's name, even if it is not done jointly, is enough to settle those issues. I suspect that some have been misled by the registrars themselves. The nice distinction between establishing *primafacie* evidence of paternity such as a court would recognize on the one hand, and the court's formal recognition of it on the other, is probably hard to make clear to a couple encountering officialdom for perhaps the first time in their adult lives.

Many also are familiar with the term 'common law marriage', and assume that it has legal force sufficient to solve problems in the last two areas mentioned. It is at best a journalist's courtesy, or a convenient shorthand, to describe a relationship which has not yet developed a terminology. Even in Scotland so-called common law marriage is not an automatic process, but a state which has to be assessed and declared by the courts. It cannot be claimed unless the habit and repute of marriage has been unchallenged. If a couple, as many will often do nowadays, admit casually, 'We're not actually married, you know', then they undermine a subsequent claim of married status from the courts. They are then probably in a worse situation than their cohabiting counterparts south of the border.

Even the most recent legislation – the 1989 Children Act – makes what I believe is a discriminatory assumption in vesting parental responsibility for a child of unmarried parents with the mother alone, even though the parents may have been long time cohabitants, and have jointly registered the child. To share a joint responsibility that is recognized in law and would continue to be so after the mother's death, or their separation, the father has to apply to the courts, or complete a parental responsibility agreement in the prescribed manner. The assumption of an unmarried father's responsibility is explicitly denied on the first page of the Act. While such fathers are living with their child's mother their caring role is unlikely to be challenged, but unless they have explicitly acquired parental responsibility their position in law is not greatly different from a babysitter or childminder to whom the mother has temporarily delegated responsibility. The main difference is that they do have a duty to maintain their child, which they would have even if they were not cohabiting.[13]

Such questions of parental responsibility and inheritance can be dealt with in other ways. One way is simply by the marriage of the parties and the reregistration of the child (which should be done within three months according to the Births and Deaths Registration Act 1953. If not the Registrar General can require the necessary information to reregister the child – though I have never heard of him doing so). Another way is by means of wills, in which the mother can specify the father as the legal guardian of their child should she die. Should that happen, he might adopt the child, but while she lives he cannot do that without her losing her responsibilities.

It seems to me that the presumption of the law at this point is that unmarried fathers are irresponsible. This is a presumption, which in the case of cohabitant fathers at least seems unreasonable. If the law worked the other way, denying unmarried mothers legal responsibility in favour of the father, there would no doubt be great cries of 'sexism' and 'chauvinism.' Cohabitant fathers should be presumed responsible unless the courts declare otherwise.

To sum up, I want to recognize that a couple may have sound reason for not marrying while choosing to live together. Many such couples do show deep commitment to each other, in ways which match sociological and at times Christian criteria of marriage. But at a more mundane level they unwittingly leave themselves vulnerable. If their love is strong and genuine they should be prepared to deal with those vulnerable areas by marriage, or a series of other legal moves, since love is practical caring.

Notes

1. *Living in Sin?* p.9
2. J.R.Gillis, *For Better For Worse; British marriages 1600 to the present.* OUP Oxford 1985, p. 138ff.
3. There are a very few couples who are unable to marry because of forbidden degrees of affinity. Such laws can seem strange and at times harsh on innocent couples, and are dismissed as taboos. At root their role is deliverance from temptation. A daughter should not compete with her mother for the affection of her step-father.
4. See for example, Liz Hodgkinson, *Unholy Matrimony*, p.93 f. '. . .first of all, historically marriage has meant little more than slavery to the average woman; as marriage laws became codified, women lost all their rights'.
5. *op. cit.* p.109
6. C. Barton, *Cohabitation Contracts* Gower, Aldershot 1985. p.10
7. C. Dyer, and M. Berlins, *Living Together* 1982
8. K. Dunnell, *Family Formation 1976*, HMSO, London. This research paper is significant in that it is the first study in the UK which asked both married and single women about their pre-marital experience of intercourse and cohabitation with their future husbands or others.
9. Pratt, *op. cit.* p.10.
10. E.g. C. Barton, *op. cit.*, Jill Bowler, J. Jackson and E. Loughridge, *Living Together; you, your partner and the Law,*

Century, London 1991, A. Barlow, *Living Together; a guide to the law,* Format, London, 1991.

11. Anne Barlow, *op. cit.* ch. 4.
12. For fuller details see e.g. *Making Sense of the Children Act 1989* Nick Allen, Longman, Harlow, 1990. s.v. 'Unmarried Fathers' in index. The Act itself is heavy going!
13. Bowler *et al. op. cit.* p.20.

SEVEN

Divorce, Cohabitation and Remarriage

Though the main theme of this book is cohabitation it is impossible to sidestep the issue of divorce. I confess that I should like to, for it is a very wide issue, and I claim no special insights in this long and fraught debate. It must be discussed, however, since many of those who are cohabiting are doing so because for one or both of them there is an undissolved marriage in the background, and once the divorce is through they perhaps plan to marry. For others the hurt of a previous marriage, and the bitterness of the divorce proceedings that ended it, make up the background to their cohabitation, and marriage is unlikely to follow because of the negative associations it has for them. The same holds good for some who have seen the bitterness of a parent's divorce, and think that they will avoid those hurts by avoiding marriage.

Still others view cohabitation as less tying than marriage, but are likely to find that if their relationship breaks up there are still unresolved matters of property which need to be sorted out. Without the protection and regulation which the divorce laws offer to those who have been married, cohabitants are likely to find their break-up as messy and hurtful as the legal business they sought to avoid.

There remains also a conundrum for those who insist on the indissolubility of marriage and regard remarriage after divorce as wrong. It is not unlike the conundrum faced by clerical lawyers in the twelfth century, in determining whether a marriage *in facie ecclesiae* was valid if it had been preceded by a clandestine or customary marriage to a third party. Popular opinion appears to have regarded the clandestine arrangement as dissoluble; the popes likewise insisted that consent, once given could not be set aside because of some later, more suit-able match. The conundrum is this – if it is wrong to dispose of a long-standing spouse in favour of another spouse, can it not be wrong to dispose of a long-standing cohabitant partner in favour of a spouse?

The link between divorce and cohabitation

Karen Dunnell's work showed clearly the relation between divorce and cohabitation. In her samples fewer than one in ten women even in the most recent year-group to get married for the first time (those between 1971 and 1975) had cohabited before marriage. By contrast, of those who had divorced and remarried, thirty per cent – about one in three – had cohabited before the second marriage. Further, of those who had separ-ated or divorced just over half had found a new relationship after six years which in two thirds the cases had become a mar-riage, but in one third was cohabitation. The most obvious rea-son for this is that the couple were prevented from formal marriage immediately because the divorce had not yet been granted. In other cases it was because of initial uncertainty about the particular relationship, or about the risks of commit-ment in general. This does not indicate, however, that the new, technically adulterous, relationship had been the immediate cause of the breakdown of the first marriage. In some cases that was undoubtedly true, but not inevitably. Dunnell also found that the mean period between the separation of the first part-ners and the beginning of a new relationship was in the region of twenty months.[1] The costly process of divorce may not have been started immediately upon separation.

In my own experience in talking with couples who wish to marry after divorce it is often only when the new serious part-ner comes on the scene that divorce proceedings are considered, even though the first marriage faltered five or ten years before. Perhaps my sample is self-selecting in favour of those whose first marriage was not split by adultery with the proposed partner. Such couples sense that their request for remarriage in church would be turned down – it certainly would by me if the circumstances became clear – and so do not ask. But I suspect that in most cases the break came first. Though not conclusive, the statistics of the grounds for divorce illustrate this point; only a quarter of decrees granted to the wife, and just over two fifths of those granted to the husband, were on grounds of adultery over the period of 1975-89. Women applied for over two and a half times more divorces than men.[2]

In more recent work by Haskey and Kiernan[3] it appears that one in eight unmarried men and one in six unmarried women between sixteen and fifty-nine were cohabiting, but that among the divorced or separated one in three men and one in four women were cohabiting. Their sample years were 1986 and 1987. They also indicate that those who had been divorced among their sample of cohabitants had lived together longer than those who had never married. (Median periods being thirty-five months for men and thirty-seven months for women as opposed to twenty-two and twenty respectively). They associate this with high levels of cohabitation among the divorced, and a decline in the rate of remarriage. The motives behind this may be the desire for greater independence, and a greater sense of caution among those who have been bound in marriage before. It may conversely reflect the greater commitment to a partnership among those who have lost one committed relationship already, whereas younger, hitherto untied, individuals are more likely either to marry or to split.

Having linked divorcés with a high rate of cohabitation, it should be pointed out that these statistics are not deterministic. Cohabitation is not an inevitable consequence of divorce, and I know of couples who clearly and conscientiously chose to remain apart until their (second) marriages. If thirty per cent of Dunnell's second marriages were preceded by cohabitation, then seventy per cent were not. If thirteen per cent of bachelors in 1986 were cohabiting, then eighty-seven per cent were not.

The other significant link between cohabitation and divorce

is, as we have seen earlier, the greater risk of divorce when the marriage began with cohabitation. Haskey's study in 1992[4] indicated that of those marrying in the early 1980s, divorce was fifty per cent more likely after five years and sixty per cent more likely after eight years among those who had cohabited with each other beforehand than among those who had not. Other studies produce similar results. One in Canada suggests a similar fifty per cent greater risk; one in Sweden eighty per cent, though since it is alleged that ninety-nine per cent of Swedes cohabit at some stage in their lives, one wonders where they got their control sample. Perhaps that finding should be stated in reverse; in Sweden the minority who do not cohabit before marriage have almost twice as good a chance of staying together.[5] In all these cases the mere fact of cohabitation is not necessarily the determining factor in the subsequent divorce; the attitude towards marriage and social conventions in general which made cohabitation an acceptable option for the couple will be more significant.

Thus an argument against cohabitation on the grounds that it correlates with a higher likelihood of divorce is flawed. What is wrong is the attitude to commitment and the understanding of marriage that accepts both. I shall discuss later whether penalizing the cohabitant or divorcé is the best way to change this attitude. However, it is worth noting in this connection that marriage in a Register Office is also more likely to be followed by divorce than marriage in a church. Haskey puts this down to both attitudes and the degree of family and community support for a couple married in a church.

It may be helpful to give some idea of the size of the question in raw figures rather than percentages. In England and Wales in 1989, 185,000 divorce petitions were filed, and 151,000 decrees absolute were eventually granted. That represents 12.7 per thousand married people. Haskey and Kiernan in 1987 estimated that there were 900,000 cohabiting couples, with over 400,000 dependent children. About thirty-four per cent of the individuals cohabiting were divorcés.

The argument against divorce on the grounds that it is bad for the health of the individuals divorced, and their children's health, educational achievement and emotional stability, is emotive, and needs to be handled carefully. That is especially so when the next part of the argument stresses the cost of the resultant health-care. If ill health is to be prevented – as it should be – the motive should be the welfare of the individuals, not the benefits to the exchequer. The same is true if these facts are adduced as an argument against cohabitation, on the grounds that cohabiting couples split even more readily, and have a less stable relationship than married couples. The deduction from that fact should perhaps be that we should attempt to make cohabitation more stable by making the relationship less easy to walk away from, rather than attempting to make it less easy to maintain or convert into a marriage that will last. Ted Pratt does this[6] referring to the work of Jack Dominian and others. My argument is not with the facts, but the conclusions based on them. But even the facts are not without contradiction.[7] Divorce, single parenthood and responsibility for second families is often related to poverty, and it may be the poverty rather than the divorce itself which gives rise to some of the problems. In any case, the fact that divorce is harmful, morally and physically, does not stop it happening. We may preach against it, and counsel to avoid it, but we still have to deal fairly with those who go through it, and those who escape it.

Divorce and the Bible – Jesus and the Old Testament

This leads on to discussion of the biblical material on divorce. Perhaps the clearest statement, and the one to start from, is that of Malachi. 'I hate divorce, says the Lord . . .' This is linked with a denunciation of violence, as if divorce is somehow itself an act of violence to the ageing wife, for the context appears to be that men were divorcing older wives in favour of younger women, possibly from outside the Jewish faith. It is also linked with an expression of God's desire to see godly offspring, as if

Malachi had noted the same unruliness among the children of divorce as has exercised modern moralists. Early in the next chapter – but part of the same oracle – God's concern for justice for hireling, widow and orphan, is expressed too. All this is linked with a warning against calling evil good, though this seems to refer to the whole of the chapter and not just to what is said about divorce. Anyone who seeks to *commend* divorce in the face of this statement needs to be very sure of his ground.

In the Old Testament divorce was not regarded as an impossibility. Nowhere is it actually commanded or legislated for, but it is more a matter of toleration of an existing practice, rather than a specific provision. In that respect, in fact, it is like marriage, which is everywhere assumed but nowhere defined. In both cases what we do find is discussion of specific situations. In the case of divorce, the classic text is Deuteronomy 24:1-4 (and the Revised Standard Version rendering is better than that of the Authorised/Revised Version) which does not strictly 'allow' divorce as the Pharisees claimed (Mark 10:4) but rather legislated about what a man might do with his former wife after she had remarried. In this and in Deuteronomy 22:13ff. and 28 where divorce is forbidden in certain circumstances, Moses was restricting some of the inconsiderate freedom exercised by some Israelite men towards their wives. A man who took divorce proceedings had to think about the consequences; he could not take them lightly, but had to give written evidence of what he was doing (no small effort in ancient Israel), nor could he lightly reverse them.

Why is divorce hated? Why is the exercise of this concession to human frailty restricted? I have suggested already in chapter 3 that concern for justice for the underdog – in this case the woman whose place in society left her at the mercy of the men in her life – is the underlying motive in the biblical teaching on divorce, and that Jesus' discussion of the matter is informed by that concern as well as by the overriding concern that people should understand what God's original intention had been. Thus, while he acknowledges Moses' concession for the hardness of men's hearts, he criticizes the Pharisees for taking that concession as the key text on the subject.[8] The key text is God's original intention for mankind expressed in Genesis 2:24. They should not be looking for reasons to get round it. The only reason Jesus will allow is adultery (if we take Matthew's account of the debate, chapter 19:3-9) and even that is not to be taken as *requiring* divorce as the Jews then appeared to hold (cf. Matthew 1:19). But, in line with what we have seen in the previous paragraphs, even the man who divorces a wife on grounds of adultery has to think carefully about the aftermath. Jesus goes on to say that remarriage is tantamount to adultery, even if the original divorce was justified. (The text is corrupt here, in Matthew 19:9, but the same point is made at chapter 5:32, and the disciples react with some alarm to Jesus' words, implying that whatever he said was even stricter than the strict Pharisaic teaching of Shammai.) No man could use even an accusation of adultery as a means of changing wives, by this rule. There is some discussion as to whether Jesus allowed remarriage after divorce for the wife's adultery.[9] Whether that is the case or not, it was not his main point, but his whole argument assumes fairly rapid remarriage as part of contemporary divorce practice (as the standard Jewish bill of divorce explicitly permitted) and branded it as adulterous. Such rapid remarriage would probably be an economic necessity for the woman, and a matter of religious duty and personal pride for the man.

Once again, if this view of the discussion is correct, we see concern that men, who held the dominant influence in the society of Jesus' day, should not abuse their power to manipulate the divorce laws in their favour. The disciples took it as a restriction on male freedom, and Jesus himself recognized that not everyone would take it on board. My point in developing this argument is this. Jesus was dealing with the pastoral and moral issues of Palestine in his day, with reference to contemporary Rabbinic debate, but also with reference to social abuses which spawned on that debate, to the detriment of the weaker members of society. He dealt with the issue by an appeal to the principles of the creation ordinances, not primarily to legislation, which suggest that he was enunciating a principle which he wanted his followers to live up to by showing respect and responsibility towards the weak and by realizing what were the moral consequences for them of divorce. He recognized that not everyone could do so. His discussion is in Jewish terms, about moral imperatives, not metaphysical impossibilities. He deals with the abuses and protects the weak by restricting men's liberty to engage in light-hearted divorce, and by warning the rabbis not to undermine what God had joined together.

Divorce and the Bible – from Jesus to the early church

Jesus' words do not settle all our questions for us. He says nothing about desertion, violence, or religious differences between husband and wife. Thus even within the New Testament we see development and apparent contradiction of what he taught. Paul, writing from the large and cosmopolitan city of Ephesus to the church in Corinth, an equally busy crossroads of the Roman Empire, was faced with another set of marital problems. He addresses them in I Corinthians 7. Some are caused by very ascetic views, others by very libertine views within the early Christian communities. He walks a tightrope between the two, lurching now one way, now the other in an attempt to win over both to a more healthy and positively moral view. One suspects, too, that his own observations of marriage may have upset his balance a little. Within the church in resisting divorce and any excessive religious zeal which might give excuse for adultery, and in valuing celibacy, he is explicitly conscious of having Christ's teaching to fall back on. In other matters he knows that he does not have a dominical precedent (verses 12, 25). He therefore gives his own, he trusts Spirit-inspired, opinion, informed by the principles accepted in all the churches (verse 17). Specifically, he appears to allow both divorce and remarriage when a Christian is deserted or forced to leave by an unbelieving spouse – with the caveat that the Christian should neither seek nor initiate the break. His permission is strong; 'he *or she* is not enslaved'. So is his discouragement of divorce, going beyond what Jesus himself is reported to have said, in that he encourages an attempt at reconciliation (verse 11).

Later in the chapter, referring to celibacy, a rather strange form of engagement (it seems) and to remarriage after widowhood, he holds up a number of options for the Christian. Though in the light of the impending apocalyptic doom or persecution he foresaw, he advises one course of action, he permits his fellow Christians to be guided by their own conscience, in the light of the sexual drives whose strength he recognizes. He does not refer at this point to remarriage after divorce nor to cohabitation. His methodology may be instructive however. He is prepared to modify and extend Christ's teaching with his own opinion formed in the light of people's personal needs and the social situation they find themselves in, and to encourage them to work out their own responses similarly. C. K. Barratt's comments[10] on verse 11 and 15 are also helpful; '. . . Paul includes a parenthesis that shows awareness that marriages could and did break up. . . .This shows that even where Christian legislation exists it is not to be interpreted, and was not interpreted by Paul, in a legalistic manner'. '. . .the prohibition of divorce does not apply here – *a further indication that Paul is not using the precept that he quotes from the teaching of Jesus in a legalistic way'.*

Divorce and the Bible – from the early church to us

If Paul adapted Jesus' teaching in the light of the circumstances he and his correspondents faced, may we do the same? I suggest that we do anyway, whether we realize it or not, since our circumstances are different from those of first century Palestine or Corinth. Some of the problems are the same. For instance, Hillel's school could stretch the meaning of 'an obscenity of a thing' (*erwath-dabhar*) to suit the wishes of the divorcing husband. Likewise the modern British concept of 'unreasonable behaviour', by far the most popular fact used to establish the breakdown of marriage, not least because it will allow an immediate petition without a term of separation, is quite an elastic concept. It may indeed include violence, but also includes far lesser allegations.

Other circumstances are different. There will still be victims of divorce, but they may not be divorced and disgraced wives, but perhaps the children of a second family, for one man's income is not likely to stretch to two household budgets, even if women are more likely to have an income of their own than in Jesus' Palestine. The rush to immediate remarriage, or even immediate cohabitation, is less likely in modern Britain; nearly half of divorced women do not establish a long-term relationship within six years of the divorce. That, at least, is the statistic that strikes me. Others are struck by the number who do enter into a new relationship within two years, and they note rightly that these relationships on the rebound (as they interpret it) are very vulnerable to further failure. The warning is timely, but even what seems to us a rapid rebound would be long by ancient standards.

Many commentators point out that the kind of separation not leading to remarriage would be most unusual in the non-Christian ancient world, yet it would be perverse to claim that these modern divorcés who delay over six years before a new relationship were all conscientiously observing Christian teaching on this matter. It is more likely that their motive is 'once bitten, twice shy', or that responsibility for children curtails their ability to meet a new partner. (Second wives, too, tend to be younger than their husbands.) The modern state's oversight of divorce proceedings, and ability to enforce or supplement maintenance payments (however reluctantly), mean that a divorced wife is not forced to seek support from another man, at moral cost to herself. Despite this the capacity for desertion is probably greater even than in Paul's Corinth at the hub of

Roman communications.

The overriding principles remain the same, however. God's intention in creation was the stable supportive union of one man and one woman, as stated in the poetry of Genesis 2. And God is offended that people create victims of their former partners or their children or of third parties through divorce and the manipulation of any secular laws that govern it. And that is so whether the manipulators are men, as I suggested would most likely be the case among those whom Jesus directly rebuked, or any other distinct group, such as lawyers, or the individual, a woman perhaps, who uses the system and her children to punish her ex-husband for his mistreatment of her.

If all this is so, how can I feel able to officiate at the weddings of those who have been divorced? Does that not amount to conniving at their sins, and actually furthering their entry into a state which is adulterous? We may well want to say, 'Neither do I condemn you', but in these circumstances can we go on to say, 'go and sin no more'? It is not sufficient to say that if we did not take their wedding here they would go elsewhere, either to another church or to a register office, or might live together unmarried anyway without the legal security that formal marriage would give them, and that therefore all I am doing by refusing their marriage is salving my own conscience. That may well be the case, but it does not justify my participation in their action. Nor is it sufficient to say that it is an opportunity to talk to the couple about what marriage means. It certainly is that, and unless that opportunity is taken there is no point in getting involved in what is at best a compromise. But that is open to the objection that our actions speak louder than our words. We may say marriage is permanent, but the fact that we are marrying again someone who has broken that permanence suggests that we do not mean it.

Getting the right message across

The trouble is that any action we take is likely to speak louder than our words. We may say that we refuse the request because we want to uphold marriage as an institution; the couple hear us saying that we are unwilling to uphold them as they institute a new phase in their lives; we may say we value marriage, and the couple say that is what they want, rather than the uncertain cohabitant state that has been theirs for some years. We say we believe in grace and forgiveness, and the couple's family and friends register that we have refused to accept them and are enforcing a whole load of rules and have forgotten that the sabbath was made for man, not man for the sabbath or any other rule book. Or we say we will marry them, and other people hear that the church is soft on divorce, does not support them as they struggle with a hard marriage themselves, and does not care that relationships go wrong. That may be rhetorical, but it expresses the dilemma which exists whichever policy is adopted generally, or whichever decision is taken in an individual case.

I defend my decision to consider marrying divorcés who may ask on the grounds that grace and forgiveness are in the end the most important principles in Christian conduct, and I would attempt to explain that to the couple. I see the risk of misunderstanding by them, or others in the community, which that involves. In relation to the couple and their marriage that involves questions about the past and their present understanding of marriage, but looks towards the future, for forgiveness is to be the basis of future reconstruction, rather than just the erasure of past sins. But I am also aware that it is possible to treat the whole discussion with the couple as a series of hoops to be jumped through. If that became the case, it would be the best hoop-jumpers whose weddings I took, not those who had learned most from their past. That was a dilemma faced by the Standing Committee of General Synod in their discussions in 1981-3 about the official authorization of second marriages after divorce in church. They rightly wanted some investigation of the couple's history and character, and an assurance that obligations to the first marriage were properly discharged (e.g. maintenance payments).[12] It seems to me that this is one way of discharging the biblical responsibility to care for the underdog – the widow and the orphan – by attempting to see that they are properly supported. As a result of this and subsequent discussion in Synod, draft questionnaires were prepared, and guidelines for those who might interview these couples. The process then foundered on complexity. I have copy of that draft questionnaire – seventeen A4 pages long. With that we would have ended up remarrying only professional bureaucrats.

Talking to divorcés about remarriage

Nevertheless, I do ask questions. What were the circumstances, and how long ago, was the original breakup of the first marriage? I am more concerned about the original split than the legal divorce, because often the cost of that only seems worth paying if legal divorce is needed to enable the second wedding. What arrangements have been made for children, if any, and maintenance? When did the present couple meet? These questions are designed to meet the points mentioned in the previous paragraph. They meet, too, the question of victims of divorce discussed earlier. I might also at this stage ask how much they have thought about the financial effects of the first marriage on the second. If it became clear at this stage that their adultery was the cause of their first split, I would refuse to marry them, but as said earlier, such couples seem to deselect themselves – or are canny enough not to let on.

I move on to moral and emotional issues. It is sometimes a tricky question to answer with the fiancée listening in, but I ask what the first spouse would have said had caused the breakup. What did he or she find wrong with the person sitting in front of me? And what has that person learned about himself or his own mistakes, so that he can attempt to remedy them next time round? Answers vary, of course. Some recognize their selfishness over time, for instance, or their concern to work all hours to bring in more money. Others are less conscious over what went wrong, and generalize: We just didn't get on after a while.

The answer that disturbs me most is when no blame or fault is accepted. I could challenge such an answer; the fault may well not be 50:50, but it is highly unlikely to be 100:0. I was struck by the continental marriage counsellor and pastor Walter Trobisch, who said he remarried only guilty parties – the ones who knew that they had contributed to the original problems and were willing to work at getting their behaviour right.[13]

I move on to discuss ways in which they may have been hurt in the past, and how those hurts may carry over into the present relationship; will they react badly to an innocent remark or request because it has touched a nerve that the previous spouse exposed? This is difficult ground, because it can sound as if I am blighting the new relationship with the old, but I think the new partner needs to recognize the danger, too, and seek to heal such wounds rather than expose them. I tell the couple that I should like to use a prayer in their service which asks for healing from such hurts. (It is printed in the appendix.) Several couples have specially asked to take it away with them for their private use. Its purpose, apart from being a genuine prayer for wholeness, is to acknowledge publicly that the church and the couple are not pretending that the past has not happened, without insisting on some major act of confession. That might be appropriate, but its place would be private. All this is in addition to what I would normally want to say about commitment in marriage, and God's grace in support, both in the private preparation discussions, and in the public service.

Promoting the well-being of divorcés

Regular marriage guidance counsellors might wish to add to these points, or indeed be horrified that I should raise them in this way. Those who disagree on ethical or theological grounds with the remarriage of divorcés during former spouse's lifetime are unlikely to be convinced that this either meets their objections, or will uphold marriage. But since a marriage is almost certain to take place, it is better that some attempt be made to place it on sure foundations. Even Cornes has an interesting section which discusses the binding nature of the second marriage, even though he regards the first marriage as still in existence. Starting with a quote from John Murray, he says.

> '"The parties have illegitimately pledge their troth . . . that troth is wrong but it still binds them to observance of what was contracted." In other words, they should not have married but they are married. This of course does not dissolve their first marriage, only death can do that . . . they are in a similar position to those who practise polygamy . . . (it is) valid though illegitimate'.[14]

It it not enough, however, to facilitate or berate remarriage (or for that matter cohabitation) after divorce. Even if communication with each other was defective between the couple in the first marriage, there was some companionship of some sort at some stage. That is removed, and the lack of it leaves a gap that the new relationship fills, whether it is before or after the median twenty months of the statisticians. And for those who do not form any such relationship there is perhaps loneliness and lack of any emotional support. Even in the impoverished community life of modern Britain family and friends may help, but not invariably. Some may draw away out of unease, fear of contagion, or loyalty to the other spouse. It would be straying still further from my main theme to develop this point, but it is surely an important role for the church to support such people, the more so where it expects them to forgo remarriage. This will mean sensitivity in the way 'family' services are described, to give a basic example, and also friendship and the encouragement of a support network. This will be relevant both for Christian divorcés and those with little church connection. Thought it will be clear that I do not follow Cornes in his practice over remarriage, I find his comments about such groups helpful (pp. 359-93).

Also relevant is his chapter on reconciliation (p.421ff.), which we noted here, was Paul's first instruction to Christians in Corinth faced with separation. This is to be distinguished from conciliation, which is merely a means of making the separation process less painful and expensive – a valid but less than ideal aim.[15] That reconciliation is worth pursuing is perhaps illustrated from the divorce statistics quoted earlier from *Population Trends 21*. In 1989 an estimated 185,000 petitions for divorce were filed in England and Wales, but only 152,000 decrees nisi were granted, and 151,000 decrees absolute. Though some of the fall out must be due to cost, it suggests some people had second thoughts. Cornes quotes research suggesting an even higher regret rate after the event.

In conclusion, divorce, whether followed by cohabitation or remarriage or not, represents a falling short of God's ideal. Christians, therefore, if married have an obligation not to commit adultery, nor in any other way to break up what God has put together; if separation does develop, they have an obligation to seek reconciliation and should not welsh on responsibilities to support even if reconciliation proves impossible. In that case I believe Paul's 'she or he is not enslaved', does permit divorce and possible remarriage. The same obligation rests upon non-believers, though the motivation may be different, since marriage is a creation ordinance before it is in any sense a Christian sacrament. Where remarriage is proposed (after a period of cohabitation or without it) I believe it is right to give the new relationship as supportive a start as possible through counselling and a Christian service. Since I take the view that the 'permanence' enjoined for marriage in the Bible is not a metaphysical state, but a moral instruction to make the relationship last if humanly (and by God's grace) possible, I do not find it inconsistent to affirm that teaching of lifelong commitment at the wedding of those who have failed to live up to the possibilities on a previous occasion.

Cohabitation followed by marriage to someone else

I began this chapter with a conundrum. Does prior cohabitation with a third party constitute an impediment to marriage? That is not a trick question to bring a stricter attitude to remarriage into disrepute, as Cornes suggests it might be.[16] If I take some cohabitations seriously I cannot simply say that they never happened or do not matter. In legal terms it does not represent an impediment. If what I have said about remarriage is valid it does not represent a moral barrier in itself, even if the cohabitation was stable and committed enough to merit consideration as a marriage. A moral barrier may, however, exist in that responsibilities are not being met and the walking away was too easy. In practical terms the previous relationship is unlikely to be mentioned in any application for marriage in church, and so no discussion or counselling is likely to take place about how and why it broke up and the emotional baggage that may be carried forward into the marriage from it. (The same is of course true of any other casual sexual relationships.) In moral terms the person's understanding of marriage and permanence is likely to have been undermined by his or her experience of cohabitation, even more so than in the case where the marriage is developing out of the couple's own cohabitation. That is all the more reason to take the cohabitation seriously. A different point makes the case even stronger, since a cohabitation of (say) ten years is no barrier to marriage, whereas an ill-conceived marriage lasting ten days is. Thus I believe it is more realistic to give some legal force to cohabitation after a certain length of time or with certain contractual commitments, than to pretend that it has not taken place. It could be consistent with this view, I believe, to campaign at the same time to persuade people not to cohabit, though some would disagree.

Notes

1. K. Dunnell, *Family Formation 1976* p. 87, p.8ff.
2. *Social Trends 21* HMSO 1991, pp.40, 41.
3. J. Haskey and K. Kiernan, 'Cohabitation in Great Britain – characteristics and estimated numbers of cohabiting partners', in *Population Trends 58 (Winter 1989)* HMSO. pp.23-32.
4. J. Haskey, 'Pre-marital cohabitation and the probability of subsequent divorce', in *Population Trends 68 (Summer 1992)* pp.10-19.
5. Cited in M. DiCanio, *Encyclopedia of Marriage, Divorce and the Family. s.v.* Cohabitation. The reinterpretation is mine.
6. *Living in Sin?* p.12f. He does not raise the issue of cost, though it has been raised in political discussion about declining morals and a return to 'basic values' in connection with single parenthood, deprivation and crime. Such arguments are essentially utilitarian and consequentialist, and I am suspicious of myself, as of others, when I use them. It seems somehow improper to argue, 'God says this, and by the way, the statistics about what happens if you don't do it prove him right'. That said, his commands are given for our good; '. . . that it may go well with you and you may live long . . .' is a consequential motive. Similar points are to be found in 'Less Quickie, More Easie,' by David Mitchell in *Third Way* Sep. 1991 vo.14/7 p.23ff.
7. DiCanio, for instance (*op. cit.*, s.v. Cohabitation) refers to research which highlights instead the deleterious effect of living in an unhappy marriage – but that is less easy to identify and quantify statistically. I should also like to hear comparison not just between divorcés and their children and a control sample of the general population, but between them and a control sample of those whose family had been split by bereavement or some other crisis. I also wonder whether poor health and mental instability represent a cause rather than a consequence of marital breakdown, so I would ask whether the medical history of the sample proper to the breakdown was studied. Having said that, I stress than I do not particularly want to disagree with Pratt on this point, but I do want his argument and mine for encouraging stable relationships to be based on the surest foundations. A

report by the British Policy Studies Institute in January 1994 also discusses this point.

8. For this point see Jay Adams, *Marriage, Divorce and Remarriage in the Bible*, Zondervan, Grand Rapids, 1980 p.64, though Adams is wrong, I think, in blaming Hillel for taking Moses' discussion of a specific case as permission for divorce. Such would be a normal deduction in rabbinic exegesis of the Bible.

9. Cf. A. Cornes, *Divorce and Remarriage* Hodder & Stoughton, London 1993 pp.209-220.

10. *A Commentary on the First Epistle to the Corinthians* A & C Black, London 1968 *in. loc.*

11. cf. Mitchell, *op. cit.*

12. *Marriage and the Standing Committee's Task* GS 571, London 1983. p.38f.

13. *I Married You*, IVP.

14. *Op. cit* pp.401-403.

15. Mitchell, *op. cit.* & M. Appleton, 'Divorce Conciliation' in *Third Way* vol.14/9, Nov. 1991.

16. Cornes, *op. cit.* p.39.

EIGHT

What is Society to Do?

Cohabitation is a legal matter. That may not be the cohabitants' intention nor the conscious decision of lawyers or Parliament, but even from the most casual and short-term relationship consequences follow which may, and perhaps ought to come to law. We have already noted that marriage clarifies inheritance and parental responsibility, while cohabitation does not. Such differences lead to difficulties and injustice if something goes wrong.

A penalty for immorality?

It might be argued that that is all to the good. A condition which is (it is said) immoral ought not to receive legal support, but should be made as uncomfortable as possible for those who indulge in it. Those who chose not to involve the law in their relationship by marrying ought not be given its benefits by the back door. On the contrary, if it is public policy to support 'the family' because of the personal and social benefits that it brings, then legal and financial arrangements that the state makes ought to be biased in favour of marriage rather than rewarding a more casual approach.

It is easy to set up 'straw men' and then knock them over, and those who maintain these views would probably state and defend them more vigorously. I do not think, however, that their premises necessarily lead to the conclusions they draw. Firstly, I have been arguing that not all cohabitations are immoral, though I would suggest that they are imperfect or incomplete. But let us grant that they are immoral. Does that justify the penalization of those who are involved? I shall deal later with the role of the law in this, but for the moment let me answer with another question; who are those involved and who will suffer from the penalization? We have already seen that it is the children who are as likely to suffer from a cohabitancy as their parents. Is it just that as a matter of public policy their teeth are to be set on edge along with their father's? When righteousness exalts a nation that kind of question has to be asked alongside questions of sexual morality, and the path of righteousness will travel between the two. And there is a second question; since a fair number of those who cohabit think that they are somehow covered by the law, and are ignorant of its gaps, is it right to penalize ignorance? The catchphrase 'ignorance of the law is no excuse' does not apply here, I suggest, since we are dealing not with criminal law but personal rights. Though the analogy is not entirely parallel, we do not deny a person the protection of the divorce laws on the grounds that 'she should have known he was a scoundrel. Serves her right!'

As regards public policy towards 'the family,' that is in fact a two-edged argument. We saw earlier that about 400,000 children are involved with the 900,000 cohabiting couples there are in this country at present. They are families, too. Public policy should support them as well as those who are in formally married families. It may be that the best way to support them is to encourage the parents to marry, so that some incentives such as the present married persons' tax allowance are appropriate. But making cohabitation more stable, and making it less easy to walk away from, is another means to this end. For this reason I believe legal reform to give it greater recognition is justifiable. We have already noted how Christians attempted in the third century, and in the twelfth, to give greater strength to unions which were at the time legally questionable or denied.

The role of law

We should first consider what role the law plays in this and other moral issues. Firstly, I suspect it introduces a confusion. To the layman who has little to do with the technicalities of the law, its most prominent feature is that it is something that you can break. By speeding or theft you break the law. The fact that the law is created to protect other people is probably less prominent in our thinking; do the drivers who speed through the thirty m.p.h. zone in Moss Side consider first the local residents for whose safety the restriction was imposed, or the officer of the law who may intercept them? I suggest that this sense of the law carries over into the perception of marriage law that some people have. Not to get married is somehow to break the law. Though that is not in fact the case, it is subconsciously perceived as a threat. But what the marriage and related laws are is a means of ordering relationships, rather than penalizing offenders. Though they contain penal clauses, against the fraud involved in bigamy or falsifying the registers, for instance, they are there to be used positively, rather than to be kept or broken.

Such a view has not always been the case, nor is it so in all cultures. Muslim law in some countries is applied to penalize adultery. The laws of the Saxon kings of England did likewise, and the Domesday survey of the Earldom of Chester records that customary fines could be imposed for fornication at different rates within and outside the city limits. It is possible that such laws have never been repealed, but I do not know how seriously the Cheshire Bench would take the suggestion that they fine someone ten shillings (or was it pence?) for this offence. No one is suggesting, so far as I know, that extra-marital relations be criminalized. That is not my point. What I am challenging is the tacit assumption that because a law is not being used, that lack of use is a breach of it that merits a penalty

It is perhaps worth remarking at this point that English law is one of the most stringent in the ways in which it regulates marriage, though that probably does not affect the assumption that I have just noted. We specify time (8.a.m. – 6.p.m.), and except in unusual circumstances place (a registered building of some kind); we require an authorized person to be present, and insist on quite a lengthy delay before the ceremony can take place (twenty-one days' notice, or fifteen days' residence). Other jurisdictions are stricter, but many are not; the American commentator, DiCanio, seems surprised that there are some States in the USA which expect as much as five days' notice.

More seriously, in this issue, law may be used as an instrument of public policy and education, or it may be used to regulate a practice so as to promote fair treatment and safety, or to control abuse. Thus the laws on racial hatred and discrimination are intended to reassure minorities that the State will protect them, to ensure that all are treated equally in matters of employment, housing and the like, and to educate the whole community in the values of tolerance and co-operation which are essential in a multifarious society. (Whether they succeed is not at issue here.) These aims are effected in this case by means of criminal or civil sanctions, and by enabling expenditure on projects which promote good relations – the legal stick and the financial carrot both serve the ends of education. Traffic regulations control the abuse of what is otherwise a good thing. They have been shaped by practical requirements and adapted to what people expect and tolerate without allowing total disorder. Thus the initial red flag rules became impractical and lost credibility. They were replaced by a speed limit in some places and deregulation in others, and now we have a range of different limits tailored to road conditions, with even the top speed regulated to 70 m.p.h. Thus the regulations retain credibility and people are protected from their own or others' folly. The laws about inheritance after intestacy, or the protection of dependents after death, represent attempts to promote fair treatment for the weak or unjustly handled, as do those about property in connection with matrimonial proceedings. It is, of course, these laws about the protection of those who are married and their children which deal most closely with the situation faced by cohabitants.

I have spoken about the proposal that disincentives should be put in the way of cohabitants; suggestions not only include the removal of tax incentives such as the old double mortgage tax relief, but also the prevention of tenancies for unmarried couples, and a policy by judges not to create case law which enhances the security of cohabitants. This withdrawal of the recognition which already exists for this pattern of relationship would be retrogressive. It might discourage one form of moral problem, but it would increase the social problem of homelessness and reward those who exploit the love or naïveté of their partners. That is to encourage another moral problem.

Another option might be to do nothing, and hope that the situation will resolve itself. In practice that does mean some change, if only because of the tendency of judges to consider matters of fairness and moral justice as well as narrow interpretation of the words of the law. Thus Lord Justice Griffiths could accept that cohabitants be treated like spouses in connection with the beneficial interests in a shared home if their relationship was intended to involve the same degree of commitment as a marriage.[1] Also, as particular areas of legislation are revisited by Parliament, they are likely to take cohabitation into account in the new provision of the law. This, however, leaves us with a rather uncoordinated pattern of legislation in a rapidly growing field, and that pattern includes, it seems, contradictions such as the status of cohabiting fathers, who cannot adopt their children unless the mother relinquishes them, must maintain them, and have to go to court to be responsible for them. I therefore agree with Chris Barton[2] in thinking that some degree of recognition and regularization of cohabitancy is needed, and believe that there are Christian as well as legal reasons for accepting this.

Reforming the law

Some of the objections to tightening the legal situation of cohabitants derive from those who opt out of marriage deliberately. They want to avoid legal frameworks and have autonomy over their own relationships, and resent the dependence they see created between the partners, particularly the dependence of women on men, in marriage. It must be said that such conscientious objectors who are able and willing to articulate their views are rare. It would nevertheless be possible to meet their objections, and perhaps even they should be asking for some reform. If they are conscientious and responsible they may well have drawn up not only wills which benefit their partners and their children in the ways they wish, but also some form of agreement or contract governing their relationship and their property. The law as it stands is very ambivalent about such contracts. It is held, on the basis of very old case-law, that they may be invalid because they link financial provisions and sexual services and so are deemed immoral; because they restrict the freedom of the partners to marry with another; because they may be contributing to the breakdown of a marriage, or because they conflict with the public policy enshrined in Lord Hardwicke's and subsequent Acts that 'marriages' may not be contracted otherwise than in the prescribed way. It seems to me that such relationships pose no more threat to 'marriage' (either Lord Hardwicke's version, or the Christian sacrament) if their legal validity is recognized than they do now, and that recognition may add greater security to the family life of the people involved. Such contracts should be recognized except if they conflict with an existing marriage, a court order, for maintenance for instance, or with the general law (to give an extreme example, over forbidden degrees of relationship). Where it turns out that one is deficient, its gaps might be made up with reference to the relevant family law. Where such a contract exists it should be held to legitimize the children, and give parental responsibility to the father.

I have no wish to glorify relationships which are deliberately uncommitted, short-term, exploitative and casual, and though these may at times be termed cohabitation they are not primarily the subject of this book. The problem comes in defining when a short-term relationship becomes long-term, and I come to that below. Existing laws on the maintenance of children, and against sexual abuse and perhaps fraud or obtaining sexual services by deception cover this situation. Some women's groups might wish to see the law, or at least legal practice, over rape and domestic abuse tightened.

Cohabiting couples who are engaged already have some of the protection that married couples do in connection with major joint purchases, such as their house.[3] They have that protection by virtue of the engagement to marry, not the cohabitation. Since so many who cohabit are doing so before marriage and have agreed on the marriage first, this partly provides the safety net for which I have been asking, and the provision offers a precedent for further extension of the protection. But many cohabit for some time before coming to an agreement to marry, and there must be times when the agreement, though in the air, has not been made definite. 'I always thought we would get married', is a rather weak case to present in court. I would have thought that the extension of this provision would be a minimal concession to cohabitants and their potential problems. But that would only be a minimum, for though disputes over property are the most common form of legal wrangle between ex-cohabitant partners, there are other areas where women and children can be exploited or left vulnerable after a change of heart.

If that is so for those who have planned a marriage, it is more so for those who have no such explicit plans (though there may be dreams). These may be described as committed but ignorant. They have not thought about what might happen if they break up, or one dies. That would be unromantic, and might threaten the relationship. They do not understand that love, truly, includes severely practical things like making a will and considering assurance and insurance policies, but think that everything will be all right, or that somehow 'common law marriage' will cover their circumstances. That is not so, and the remedy for their situation lies partly in better information being made available in schools and the community generally, and partly in their own action, if they realize their vulnerability, in making wills or regularizing their relationship. That being said, ignorance will continue, and I believe we should legislate for ignorance.

Common law marriage?

The analogy of common law marriage is helpful. I know there are differences; in common law marriage in those places where it is recognized it is required that the couple live together with the present intention of being husband and wife without denying their public reputation of being married, whereas the present intention (it is alleged) of cohabitation is that they avoid marriage.[4] That may be correct in some cases, such as the conscientious objectors mentioned earlier, but often the situation is more complex. A couple will affirm among their immediate community that they are husband and wife, but when they fill in 'official' returns such as voter registration, they reveal their unmarried status by using separate surnames, because 'You must use your official name on an official form'. Of Dunnell's respondents, two per cent of those who described themselves as 'married' later turned out to be cohabiting, and others who admitted not to have been through a marriage ceremony regarded themselves as married. (*op. cit.* p.5.) Others will say, 'we're not actually married', meaning, 'we haven't actually been through a formal ceremony', while asserting in the same breath their commitment to each other, or their belief that 'It doesn't make any difference in the end, does it?' It is such people as these who need the same solutions as the law provides for statute law marriages if their relationship runs into difficulties or disaster strikes. Further, their relationship exists and works even if less than ideally; it is unrealistic for the law to pretend that it does not, and such unrealism is unjust.

It is objected that definitions are unclear and the dividing line blurred between stable and uncommitted relationships. That is true whether you are talking about common law marriage or cohabitation, but the uncertainties are there in existing law already (as the judgement of Griffiths LJ suggests) and the potential for injustice remains. In fact in this country the DSS manage with a working definition of cohabitation, albeit in connection with payments in the fortnight in question, while many jurisdictions live with common law marriage. DiCanio notes that thirteen American states recognize it. Though it is justified on the grounds that the officials who can conduct a wedding may be a long distance from the couple's home that can only be a historical explanation; Washington DC, the nation's capital, also recognizes it. She reports that there is a campaign to remove such provision from the law books – led by insurance companies who want to remove the possibility of multiple claims, and demographers, who cannot cope with it in their statistical surveys. It is defined by consent, common abode and exclusive sexual relations, and by undenied habit and repute in the couple's home community. Length of time together is corroboration, but not proof of the existence of the marriage, and intercourse consummates an expressed or implied intention to marry. We can see in that echoes of the pre-Hardwicke situation in England. Some states insist on all these conditions others take them as corroboration of an alleged marriage. Such a common law marriage can be dissolved only by legal divorce or death, and not by any kind of common law divorce. The existence of such an institution does not in itself diminish the value of regular marriage, any more than it does in Scotland.[5]

Other legislations have faced up to the problems posed by cohabitation, specifying certain types of cohabitation as being parallel to marriage. In South Australia, for instance, inheritance after an intestate death can be claimed by declaration of the courts if there has been a four-year cohabitancy, or a child has been born of the union. A proposal from Tasmania that marriage would be recognized if dependency could be proved serves the purpose of protecting someone left in difficulties by the partner's death, but does not meet the objections of those who feel that dependency is degrading (any more than less radical provision in the British Inheritance (Protection of Dependents) Act does) and it leaves the question unresolved if the survivor has equal or greater resources.

A possible reform proposal

Given that other jurisdictions can cope with the difficulties of recognizing marriage-like cohabitation, I believe that it is possible here. The purpose of such a move would be the protection of the vulnerable, and also as an affirmation that 'walking away is' not 'easy'. As such I believe it could enhance rather than diminish the institution of marriage by educating people in the seriousness of their relationships. But it would not be sufficient to declare that all cohabitation constitutes marriage. Criteria are needed. In what follows I offer an idea of how these might be defined. I offer it in some ways as an 'aunt sally', a discussion document to be critized and refined. It is modelled, in fact, on the present divorce law, in mirror image. That may be a criticism in itself, since that law is currently under review, but there is certain neatness in this reciprocity. The first point to make is that where one or both of the parties are committed to an existing marriage, cohabitation cannot dispense with that commitment. Responsibilities such as the first wife's pension rights cannot be ducked. If that marriage is not to be rescued, then its end must be sorted out as justly as possible[6] taking into account the moral views as well as the practical needs of the first spouse before new commitments can be recognized.

The present law is that after one year of marriage a petition for divorce may be filed if the marriage can be alleged to have broken down on grounds of 1) adultery, 2) unreasonable behaviour, 3) desertion for two years, 4) separation for two years (with mutual consent) or 5) separation for five years on the request of one party. For that reason I suggest the basic requirement of the legal recognition of this sort of relationship should be one year of common residence as if husband and wife. (Perhaps longer would be better, but I am using the divorce law as a template.) The implication of this is that the relationship should be sexually exclusive, though this would leave a loophole for those who want to be able to walk away easily, in that a contrived one-night stand could frustrate the intention of the law. Given this basic prerequisite, 1), the birth of a child conceived within that period of cohabitation should be grounds for regularzing the union. This would deal with the anomalies to do with legitimacy and parental responsibilities.

Also given that basic prerequisite, 2), it seems reasonable that a promise or engagement to marry, followed by physical consummation, should be accepted as initiating a regular union, even if that is celebrated and ratified publicly only later. An implication of this is perhaps that the completion of a 'banns form' or other legal notice of intention to marry takes on a greater significance and would need to be done by both parties – though there are other valid ways of making one's intention clear. This extends the existing protection in connection with joint property (though even that is somewhat complex), and corresponds to the old concept of marriage *per verba de futuro* followed by consummation. Though similar to the old ideas expressed in action for breach of promise, which became obsolete in 1970, this deals with the security of a deserted or bereaved party, not the hurt feelings of a jilted one.

3) When a couple signify their commitment to each other through mutual wills, pooling of finances, the nomination of each other in insurance or assurance schemes that should be taken as evidence corroborating their union. They have planned their futures on the basis of their relationship, as a married couple do, and the dissolution of that relationship leaves them equally vulnerable. They need the same solutions to those difficulties as a married couple would. I talk about corroborating evidence, because I do not think it appropriate that these provisions should come into force automatically. It would be conceivable under those circumstances for a person to have several spouses without knowing it. But what is at issue is the definition of rights to make a claim if something goes wrong.

Thus, 4), to permit one party to the cohabitation to claim regular status for the union after five years, even if the other party did not agree, would give him or her access to the protection of family and inheritance law if threatened by desertion, or left abandoned on the death of a partner.

The fifth possibility is hardly likely to be taken up; if a couple agree to regularize their union after two years (to parallel the divorce procedure) then the obvious way to do it would be by a visit to the registrar or the vicar to arrange a wedding. It might be, however, that the desire for a simple, private affair, or the need for speed because of an impending serious operation, or call up, made a simple declaration of their existing union appropriate. What I have in mind would be similar to the process that applied in Scotland until 1940, by which a couple could register the fact of their 'irregular' marriage retrospectively on payment of a fee to the registrar. In Newfoundland it is possible for a cohabiting couple to signify that they want their relationships to be governed by the matrimonial property legislation, and are then treated as married.

We noted that the American common law marriage regulations meant that the couple could not 'divorce' each other except through the courts. On that analogy, should a cohabiting couple who have fulfilled the above criteria be forced to go through a legal 'divorce' before contracting a marriage with anyone else? Or would such a cohabitation be a valid impediment to the contracting of a further marriage even if it had never been ratified? This raises problems of proof, and publicity. I think it would be necessary for such liaisons to be declared and proof of some kind offered that they had ended by agreement or at least with all obligations met. This might well be difficult, and the lawyers may say it cannot be done. Not to consider it would be for the community to admit that walking away can be easy, and that the moral and emotional commitment created by cohabitations, as well as its financial implications, do not really matter. To do nothing is to admit that the status quo is acceptable; that you can almost do anything short of committing matrimony, and then, provided you pay maintenance for any children, forget about it and have your white wedding anyway.

Notes

1. Griffiths LJ in Bernard v. Josephs (2 WLR 1052 at p.1061) cited by C. Barton, *Cohabitation Contracts,* Gower, Aldershot. 1985 ch. 1
2 *op. cit.* ch. 8, pp. 73ff. In this chapter Barton lists eight reasons against further legal intervention in the situation of cohabitants, and twelve in favour. Some of these points have already been dealt with in legislation since 1985 and others are not significant in my discussion here, but I have found his list helpful in shaping my argument below.
3. From the Matrimonial Proceedings and Property Act, 1970.
4. DiCanio, M. *op. cit.* p 125. (s.v. Common Law Marriage).
5. In certain limited circumstances a very clearly defined and dated commitment may be necessary, for example, in immigration cases.
6. I say wife, since that is the most likely scenario. The implication of this may be that where age or infirmity mean that the first wife can only be dependent on the support she would have expected from her (ex-) husband and his state or private contributions, the future support of the second wife or family needs to be allowed for through a surcharge on the couple's NIC payments or through private arrangements. But how feasible is that and how acceptable politically?

NINE

What is the Church to Say?

The top end of the street was still a bomb site. Lower down was a row of Georgian terraced houses, 'with potential' as the estate agents would say. Their owner knew it, for he was one of the biggest landlords in Bath, and was working through his property turning it into high value executive flats. But for the moment this street was in the hands of the hippies and their communes, and as a curate I was enjoying the chance to visit and talk widely and at times deeply about the Christian faith, and people's beliefs and hopes in general. A girl, probably in her early twenties, answered the door, and invited me in. I think there were some others there too, smoking and talking. She was living with one of the men in the house, which did not surprise me; in that area cohabitation was far more common that in Karen Dunnell's nationwide sample four years later. What did take me aback was that after a while she said that her father was a clergyman in another part of the county.

Ethical issues – personal dimensions

Whenever I talk now, twenty years on, to groups of Christians about cohabitation I find that among those attending the meeting are people whose child or grandchild, or father-in-law, is living with their girl- or boy-friend or companion. And whether it is clergy or lay families involved, it is no longer just a matter for those of a rebel or Bohemian bent. Cohabitation is not just a matter of how the law should be framed to uphold family values and promote fair treatment of divorced or deserted partners. It is a matter of how I relate to my cousin, or sister-in-law. It is personal, and pastoral. That does not mean it ceases to be an ethical question, but it is very much on home ground, and not only about 'them' somewhere else. And it is a matter in which a great deal of emotional capital is invested, not just by the parents of cohabitants, but by those who resisted temptation, or regret lost opportunities, or who struggle now with a difficult marriage, or on the part of some clergy who feel that they have failed Paul's test in 1 Timothy:4, 5, of managing one's own household – despite the radical changes in families and households since then.

I spoke to our Mothers' Union group when I was preparing an earlier version of these ideas, and suggested to them that cohabitation was not as big a threat as they might think; after all, before Lord Hardwicke the church had been able to live with relationships very like cohabitation. They were not convinced. I was hoping to set the present quite narrow marriage laws in a long-term context, and allay some of the guilt by association that they felt. Some time later I saw the minutes which had been kept of that meeting. The secretary had noted 'we all preferred the old ways', by which she clearly meant what they had grown up with in the 1920s-1940s. Nevertheless, the fact that it had been discussed openly, and she and other members had been able to share their views, and their worries about their own families, had meant that it was a lively and supportive meeting. This is one thing that the Church can do, not solving the problems, but sharing the perplexity of its members as they face a rapid and threatening change in the values of those who live around them, and of some within their family circle. But providing a support group is by no means all that the Church should do.

The educational role of the church

In the previous chapter I described the possible role of the law in providing protection for the deserted or bereaved partner and children. In the course of those provisions a certain amount of education would be achieved and cohabiting parties encouraged to confirm their relationship. I see education as one of the major roles of the church in this matter, because of the established interest and high public profile it has in matters of marriage. Its means of education are its own inherent functions of preaching and shared fellowship and study; its public statements and practice in connection with marriage ceremonies; and as a by-product of its prayer and worship. It also has say in a large number of educational establishments, and ability to shape the curriculum taught in them. In a following section I have put forward ideas as to what that school curriculum might include. Chapters three and four, suitably adapted to each church's needs, offer resources for church based study.

The educational role of the law would be to draw attention to the disabilities suffered if people do not regularize their relationships. As such it is largely social and financial, though it has the moral element of forcing individuals to accept the responsibilities they incur through their sexual choices. The church's teaching will refer to these social and health problems that are related to unstable relationships. It will mention, at least among the appropriate groups, the dangers of illness inherent in casual and promiscuous sex. It will point out that all too easily a series of 'committed relationships' have become serial promiscuity, and that self-deception happens all too readily in this field. It will expose the ways in which sexuality is exploited in our economic and social life in ways which diminish a person's integrity and autonomy (the old philosophers' fear of *passio* was not entirely unfounded). It will talk about the disruption and offence that is created by adultery. But Christian ethics and general concern is more than a warning not to get hurt. Our vision is greater than utilitarian consequentialism. We have a vision to share of the positive goods of Christian marriage; trust, affection, support, care and sexual love. That may not be easy, if only because to speak or lead discussion about marriage somehow puts the speaker under a microscope in his own mind, if not that of his audience. If I say this, or that, about marriage I become conscious of how I have failed to match the ideal I uphold, conscious of the time I have not given my wife, or the support I have not given my children which I am now saying is one of the blessings of Christian marriage. Perhaps, we say, the church ought to be a place where weaknesses can be shared, and overcome; but perhaps also we find it a place where weakness is exploited. We need forgiveness for failed fellowship before we can convincingly teach forgiveness and restoration in failing marriages.

The supportive role of the church

While the law can offer a framework and a means of handling breakdown, the Christian ideal of marriage offers a quality of relationship and mutual support, and a dynamic which can, if allowed, deal with breakdowns. So while we may say (to put it simply at present) divorce is wrong, we should be wanting to say more loudly that here is the strength of the Holy Spirit to enable forgiveness and reconciliation to take place. That, in turn, leads on to the next area in which the Church has something to say – the field of support, counsel and moral guidance. If we say, individually or as a Christian organization, that the Holy Spirit is there to enable reconciliation we must be ready to put our time, resources and skills at his disposal, and be ready to back other agencies which specialize in the support of marriage and couples in difficulties.

In the matter of divorce, there is clearly a great deal of discussion and a great many pronouncements have been made, and it is not my primary aim here to add to that. From what I have already said it is clear that I do not believe divorce to be metaphysically impossible, nor in an absolute sense morally wrong. What I would want to say is that in every divorce sin is at work, whether in the attitudes of the couple concerned, the actions of one or both of them, the circumstances which they have had to live under, the machinery of the law they have got caught up in, or the social values they have imbibed. There is probably a mixture of all these in any divorce, though the individual choice to divorce is always a moral choice, whatever the surrounding pressures, and so represents a decision to unmake vows made for better or worse. No one can ever say, 'I had no choice. . .' but to initiate divorce proceedings. But after all reasonable attempts to heal the wounds and reconcile the parties – and in Christian idealism perhaps attempts beyond reason as well – occasions will remain when divorce is the lesser of two evils, and the choice will be the right one. There will also be occasions – very many of them[1] – when the divorce has gone through, but the individuals come to regret that result, and an 'end of term' report on the outcome of the reconciliation attempts that the 1969 Divorce Reform Act requires, would read 'could have tried harder'. Perhaps that point needs to be prominent in our education about divorce, cohabitation, and their consequences.

There will also be times when an end of term report would be more severe. Where the deliberate acts of one or both of the parties have undermined and ultimately destroyed their relationship there should be a moral black mark against them. In particular (in the context of this book) the adultery of one or other of them with a third party, leading to cohabitation with that third party, is sinful, whatever difficulties there were in the marriage beforehand. Whatever those difficulties, this was not the moral way to resolve them. To drift from one unsatisfactory relationship into another without attempting to repair the first is a recipe for disaster, which may be the moral and emotional background behind the high failure rate of second marriages begun rapidly after the end of the first. Nothing of what I have said elsewhere in this book about the history of irregular or informal marriage should be taken as justifying a sinful relationship such as this.

Having said this much about the balance of wrongs there may be in a divorce, we should recognize that the Church is most often asked for its involvement far too late to do anything with the first marriage. It is rather late to talk about saving the first marriage that ended five years before, when a couple are in front of you, wanting to book the date for what is the second marriage for both of them. Thank God that some couples will come to their vicar to ask for help in a rocky or stormy marriage before a final break comes, but they are a minority. Perhaps we give the impression that we would disapprove so much of them for having problems; perhaps we actually say too little about marriage from our pulpits – about its riches and its difficulties – that they don't expect us to be of use anyway. One thing that I try to do for a couple who come to me to plan a first wedding is to make them aware that they might turn to their local vicar if difficulties arise. I mention this as we look through the detailed points made in the wording of the marriage service, but I realize that amid the plethora of information and the romance of the occasion they may not take it in.

Can cohabitation be right?

Moving now to discuss what the Church should say about cohabitation, and having noted one occasion where it is clearly wrong, we should ask whether there are any occasions when we can say that cohabitation is in an absolute sense right? This is again a somewhat artificial question, because in most specific cases a couple will come to the church after the event, as their plans move towards regular marriage. It can be brought up, however, in the course of general discussions, say in a school lesson or with students or a youth group. I have implied that at times cohabitation amounts to 'common law marriage' or the irregular marriages of the middle ages. For this reason it is illustrative to refer to the discussions of canon lawyers. In a standard handbook on Roman canon law, van Vliet and Breed[2] discuss irregular marriage and record that it is accepted by the church in certain restricted circumstances. Thinking of sacramental marriage in the Roman tradition they say that the church would recognize an irregular marriage if a priest were not available within a reasonable length of time (they mention a month, and have places in mind where the Roman church is in a minority or missionary situation) or if one party seemed near death. Two witnesses would be required, and, they note, the parties should realize that the State might not recognize their union. This approach is similar to the American arguments in favour of common law marriage mentioned in chapter 8. In other words, except in very exceptional circumstances cohabitation is never in the class of absolutely right courses of action, and the answer for the wag in the youth club is that if he ever is marooned on a desert island with the girl of his dreams they may 'marry' (and cannot break it off when they get rescued), but in any other circumstances his dreams should include a formal wedding. Cohabitation is at best a second-best solution to the questions of courtship, relationship and marriage, and why, I would ask the wag in the club, does she want second best in her life and the life of the lad she says she loves?

So the question may be rephrased. Are there circumstances where second best is justified? Clearly there are some when it is not. When the motives are self-gratification or exploitation of one by the other, or even by both of each other, or when the degree of commitment involved is negligible and short-term, then that relationship is built on sin, not love in any Christian sense at all. It is lacking in the qualities we saw in Christian marriage, and in the sociologists' criteria too. The same is true if the motives are genuine on one part, but the other party is using the relationship. (Even in such a case, however, the legal provisions that I suggested in the previous chapter as means of protecting the aggrieved or exploited party should apply, however defective the intentions of the other proved to be.) In such a case the balance of sinning and being sinned against is uneven, but the whole relationship is flawed. Nevertheless in pastoral care Christians need to be aware of that balance of sin, as well as the flaw. 'We told you so!' is no real help or comfort to the single mother on benefit reduced because she is reluctant to acknowledge the father she now wants no more to do with.

Further types of cohabitation considered

At the other end of the spectrum, perhaps, come the conscientious objectors. They see sin (if they will use the word) in the institution of marriage itself and the way it operates in their society, so to involve themselves in it would be a gross lack of integrity. For such people I have respect, and if they knew me well enough I would tell them (with a grin to soften the dig) that they are married in all but name. But I would expect such people to be very conscientious, and to have shown their love and commitment to each other, or at least their respect for each other's needs and integrity, in the practical foresight found in a contract or living together agreement, and through wills or trusts that deal with their shared property, children and joint responsibilities. I would also challenge their jaundiced view of what marriage is meant to be, and their extremely individualist approach to society.

Working backwards through Dyer and Berlins' list (cited in chapter 6) we come to those whose cohabitation is an exploratory, trial relationship. Perhaps the best that can be said about this is that it is better than a trial marriage. The couple are more honest about their uncertainties, but the morally right course of action in this case should be a longer engagement apart. The scope for deception or self-deception is great; the trial is not in fact logically valid, and in terms of the emotions and uncertainties it actually creates it is not a fair trial either. There will be bonds, however, and parting will leave its scars. There are responsibilities and as with the casual cohabitants the legal safeguards proposed in the previous chapter should apply even if we insist that morally this was no marriage in any sense. At the very least they will concentrate the mind wonderfully, and prevent the trial dragging on interminably. Even if the relationship does develop into marriage, that is not the simple resolution of the matter. There may still be scars, and if problems develop, or one of the parties feels that the other's personality turns out differently from what was anticipated in the trial, there may be a feeling that they were trapped into the marriage, thus generating even greater resentment, instability and problems. (This was a problem noted by Selwyn Hughes in connection with those who simply had had pre-marital intercourse[3], but that is now so frequent that one wonders whether it is an excuse for the difficulties rather than a cause.)

Dyer and Berlins spoke of a group who are 'committed' but do not think that marriage as such is for them. They are in some ways like the conscientious objectors, though their ethical stance is less clear. Do they have any valid moral grounds for saying marriage is not for them or they are not for marriage, or is their love and commitment less than they are prepared to admit? To live with integrity together, these are questions that they have to answer to themselves and each other unless their sin is to be one of deception. In a former age the fact that the couple speak of themselves as 'committed' exclusively to each other would be tantamount to the words 'I take you as mine,' and their relationship would have been treated as an irregular marriage *per verba de praesenti,* or if the phrasing was 'We will get married . . . ' then intercourse would consummate a marriage *per verba de futuro.* They would be married, but might have found themselves required by the church courts (acting for the state) to ratify this *in facie ecclesiae.* As with the 'trialists' the legal safeguards should apply, if only to concentrate their thoughts, and the possible emotional and pastoral issues when the relationship is regularized will be similar. As with the conscientious objectors, I would look to see signs of the genuineness of their love and commitment in practical things such as mutually beneficial wills, joint ownership of property, and the like. Love is more than hitting it off with one another even if that means boring things like seeing a solicitor.

There are some people, and I am not sure whether they should be thought of as 'committed' or 'trialists' or even the first of Dyer's categories, 'married'. These have causes in their own personal histories for walking very slowly towards marriage. Previous experience of a violent husband, or the tragic death of a wife, leave them both wounded and wary. They need emotional support, and rightly or wrongly feel that they have found it in the person with whom they cohabit, but are maimed by the fear, expressed or subliminal, that in marriage it would all happen the same way again. Bowler and her colleagues call them 'battle-scarred divorcés'. These, of all people, need pastoral support and understanding to help sort out their mixed and at times irrational emotions. Jesus' gentle dealing with the Samaritan woman is a model of how to meet them, though her circumstances were not quite the same. In such circumstances especially I find it helpful to think of Christian marriage not as a mould into which we must all be pressed instantly, but a destination to which we journey. The battle scarred may well be on the way there, but they are walking wounded. They are vulnerable, and may well be more sinned against than sinning.

The same might be said of those who defer their formal wedding, but live together while they wait for it. A whole range of reasons lie behind such a choice. The degree of blame, and the balance of wrong varies according to the reasons. If it is simply the couple's sexual impatience, we may ask why they are delaying the wedding. If they are waiting till they or the family can afford to give them a good send off, or until the desired location for the reception is free to be booked, we may ask whether their sin is not ostentation and pride as much as lust. We may also say that society is at fault in creating the impression that a wedding must be a grand and showy affair.[4] There was perhaps something to be said for the old 'penny weddings' of the pre-Victorian working classes, in which the whole village or the whole street would contribute to the celebration of the couple and their good luck. The modern expectations would be hard to break, though some couples do achieve a 'quiet wedding'. Is there any mileage in the church actually encouraging a modern form of 'clandestine marriage', (not mere 'betrothal' which solves nothing) in which the legalities and the 'sacramental' element are dealt with quietly after minimal notice and with minimal fuss, on the express understanding that there will be a return to the Church for a major 'celebration of the marriage' of N and N followed by a reception, disco and any other appropriate secular paraphernalia on the first anniversary, when everyone has saved up for it?

In such a celebration it should be understood that the family is involved, even if it understands that the major celebration is to follow. Marriage that is not known among the family and peers to the couple (even if all the correct legal procedure has been followed) somehow lacks one of the elements of Christian marriage, that the commitment should not only be before God, but also before 'this company'. I know of a couple who lived together for several years, and it only came out to the man's parents casually and accidentally one day that they had actually got married. In moral terms was that marriage? (I ask that with my tongue partly in my cheek. Answers should only be written on one side of the paper at once.) For those who fear that 'their day' will be taken over by the family, the Church should offer support. They should be encouraged to go public over their relationship, but if they do not their sin is as much to do with the broken family relations as with their sexual relationship, and the family probably share the moral responsibility. That does not make it all right, but it does help explain the wrong.

Dyer and Berlins speak of a group whom they term 'married,' that is, who will marry as soon as they are able, but are awaiting (usually) the divorce process to run its course. (I currently have another case on my books, as it were. The couple are touring Australia together, and will marry when they return to the UK where most of the family is, and where they have a stable address from which they can qualify to be married.) If the promise to marry as soon as possible is genuine, then they are in the same position as those who are 'committed' and I would expect them to vouch for their commitment in the same way, taking into account their existing moral responsibilities. If their adultery was the cause of the breakup of the first marriage, however, then their relationship cannot be other than adulterous, however happy they feel because of it. In this situation the seventh commandment strictly applies, and while the Church may look for repentance from such sin and subsequently integrate repentant sinners into the Christian community, I believe that the Church's integrity requires that they may not be married in church, even though for legal reasons their liaison needs to be regularized.

Celebrating the wedding of cohabitants

In these other situations can the Church with integrity celebrate the weddings of those who have been cohabiting? If they have not committed adultery, because no other spouse is involved, surely they have been fornicating in anticipating marriage, so that a Church wedding blesses their sin? Where the cohabiting relationship began as a casual affair, motivated by sexual opportunity rather than genuine commitment (and I realize that genuine is a slippery word which can hide self-deception) then that is true. Such a beginning is morally dubious, and only in retrospect can it be seen even as quasi-marital. The desire to move towards a regular relationship may be taken as a sign of personal realignment. Here is an opportunity both for education in what Christian marriage means, and to see that realignment in terms of repentance and forgiveness. This may not always be clearly expressed, since faith can grow slowly and fuzzily, but it may be more explicit; 'I became a Christian and realized I must get my life straight, so I married the girl I was living with at the time'. The same is true of the unions which in a former age would have been recognized as irregular. There is a lack of understanding of what the commitment of Christian marriage means, and the opportunity to reshape the couple's understanding of marriage should be taken.

That leads on to another issue. In former ages those irregular marriages, unblessed in church, corresponded in some way to modern register office weddings. A high Roman Catholic view would see these also as lacking, although Anglicans, Erastian at heart and brainwashed by the philosophy of Lord Hardwicke's Act and its 1836 successor, have accepted the State's provision uncritically. I wonder whether we should be urging people married in a register office, and now perhaps converted, to seek a church blessing for their marriages. I am not convinced that it is the State which consecrates matrimony to such an excellent picture that in it is represented Christ's marriage to his church. I say this not because I believe (with the Romans) that the absence of a priest leaves the marriage invalid, but because of the opportunity it should give to discuss and witness to the meaning of a Christian marriage, and the grace God offers to live that out. In the quality of that covenanted relationship lies the picture. The 1949 Marriage Act explicitly allows this subsequent blessing, and it should not be simply a second-best offer for those whose divorces leave their clergy uneasy about giving them a full service.

The church's role

To summarize the last few pages, if someone (Christian or non-Christian) asks me before the event whether they may just live with their partner, I would say they should not, and ask them what prevents them from committing matrimony instead? I should listen to their answer with respect, and perhaps honest criticism, while maintaining that it is second best to formal marriage and less than the Christian understanding of marriage. If they are certain of their commitment, why not marry? If they are uncertain, cohabitation will confuse the issue. But if they come to me after the event, I will again want to hear their reasons and the history of the relationship before I assume that it is sinful. I believe that we should work with them in regularizing the relationship in a Christian wedding service leading to Christian marriage.

This may sound like a double standard – like saying 'Don't, but if you do, it's OK'. That may seem so, and it is part of the compromise involved in living in a sin-scarred world, conscious that the actions of individuals and couples are affected by the sins of others as well as themselves. There is a lovely story, which should be told in an Irish accent if you are not afraid of being called racist, of an American tourist asking directions to Ballybunion. He gets the reply, 'If I were to be going there, it's not here that I would be starting from'. Maybe it is not from cohabitancy that we should like people to be starting out from on their journey towards a Christian marriage, but to walk with them gives them a greater chance of reaching that destination. If the onlooking world thinks that is a seal of approval on cohabitation, then we need to proclaim the qualities of Christian marriage at the service all the more clearly, but for many in that onlooking world the message will be the opposite; 'At last he's made an honest woman of her!'

We have seen the Church's role in teaching, and moral counsel, in pastoral support of the perplexed families or elders of those who choose to cohabit, and particularly in contact with those who ask for a church wedding. The issue of cohabitation, and marriage in general, should be part of the devotional life of the church, incorporate prayer. I make some suggestions for this in an appendix. It should also be part of the prayers of individual Christians, as they pray for their own families and friends and their future (and perhaps as yet unknown) spouses. It seems to me to be eminently biblical to pray about the way God wants the lives of our children or other family members and of ourselves to develop, and whom, if anyone, they are to marry. That need not be restricted to the family. To pray for a cohabitant couple in the street is surely part of our Christian role as members of a community of priests. And that prayer, I believe, should be that they grow and develop together in love, so that they are ready not only to get married in church, but also to let their relationship show all the qualities that make a Christian marriage. This should be especially true if they ask for their child to be baptised.

Much of what I have said so far in this chapter relates specifically to what clergy are asked to do. The appendix on a 'parish policy' amplifies this with some questions to help colleagues think through these and related issues (including leadership in the Church by cohabitants) in advance. To have a 'policy' is just that, advanced planning for contingencies, and does not imply that you have joined the politically correct brigade. It may give added weight to a decision that someone finds unwelcome, to be able to say that it is not dreamed up on the spur of the moment, and the PCC will back it. But the issue of how to react to cohabitation is not solely the prerogative of the clergy. All Christians have to relate to ambiguous or possibly immoral situations in their day-to-day lives, and this is one of them. Some feel that the way to maintain their Christian witness to the integrity of marriage requires them to distance themselves from a couple who are cohabiting, especially if they are closely related, or actually to absent themselves from the couple's wedding if they do make it to the altar. Such a course of action needs to be carefully thought through, however conscientious it is. It is all too easily misinterpreted as lack of concern, or priggishness. Worst of all it may be counter-productive, as the potential son-in-law reacts by saying to himself that he does not want to be *joined* to that family, and persists in mere cohabitation, despite intense loyalty to his partner herself. The question is acute, especially if the daughter and her partner are to visit her parental home. Does their use of the same bed there imply more than the parents can accept? Will a refusal to allow the visit distance parent and child? Does the moral imperative of loyalty within the family by parent to child outweigh the dishonour felt by father and mother as they see the fifth commandment broken against them? What are the other motives operating in the parents' thoughts alongside their Christian convictions; do they feel ashamed themselves, or less respectable, or criticized in their own relationship? Are the young people being deliberately provocative? Can the point be made in such a situation by giving the couple the chance to respect the parents' feelings, and offering them separate beds (if space permits, of course) and leaving them to react? It is a complex matter, and in this particular example it may depend how long the daughter has left home, and how long she has been cleaving to the partner. Here, seriously, are questions to be answered, perhaps in a house-group discussion, though leaders of such a group need to be alive to the possible raw nerves such talk may touch in group members whose children or grandchildren are living this way. Such discussion is never merely academic nowadays.[5]

I shall conclude by stating my own view. In the course of my life I come across all kinds of people with whom I disagree, some more strongly than others, some on religious or moral grounds, some for less laudable reasons; Jehovah's Witnesses, militants, armaments workers, petty thieves, Government ministers, pacifists, spiritualists, . . . I am confident enough in my faith to state what I believe if the opportunity arises, and to listen to them, not believing that I will be contaminated by what is wrong in their views, but hoping that what is right in mine will rub off. I approach those who cohabit in the same way, thanking God for what good their relationship represents within God's common grace to humanity, and longing for it to be enriched with the Christian elements which can make marriage a saving grace.

Notes

1. Cornes, *op. cit.* cites research in Bristol to this effect on p.413.ff.
2. *Marriage and Canon Law*, A. H. van Vliet and C.G.Breed, Burns and Oates, London 1964, s.v. Irregular Marriage.
3. *Marriage as God Intended*, Kingsway, Eastbourne, 1983, pp.15-18.
4. J. R. Gillis *For Better, For Worse*, Oxford 1985. pp. 138-43 details the development of quiet and ostentatious weddings over the years after Hardwicke's Act.
5. Other discussion starters are given in the appendices, as is a flysheet used in a parish magazine and with couples seeking their child's baptism.

TEN

A Policy for the Parish or School?

What follows is a series of questions and points that might be considered when planning how to react to cohabitation in a parish setting. I deliberately say 'parish' setting, since this is written with an Anglican parochial ministry, rather than a narrow congregational ministry in mind. The questions are not intended to be directive, thus allowing those who disagree with my conclusions to draw on the ideas.

1. Schools

(a) Curriculum

The governors of an aided school are responsible for its religious education policy and are responsible for the curriculum generally, including its sex education policy and what used to be called 'personal and social education'. The implementation of that policy is, however, in the hands of teachers who may or may not share the convictions of the governors, and they will be teaching children whose family circumstances may be far from ideal. These teachers will in their professional capacity be concerned that children do not feel criticized or disadvantaged because of these circumstances. In other schools, which may well have church members as governors appointed from the community, or as parents or staff, these curriculum areas are likewise within the responsibility of the governors, though the RE. syllabus is that agreed in a relevant local authority.

Within these limitations Christians have the opportunity to shape what is taught both in 'church' and other schools. Since most church schools serve the primary age range this opportunity is further limited by what the children can take in at that phase, but the opportunity remains. In all schools, however, governors might consider both in RE and sex education/PSE whether . . .

i. . . . Sexuality is taught as a gift of God in creation, rather than merely as a biological function;

ii. . . . it is taught as something with moral as well as physical implications to do with human relationships;

iii. . . . those relationships are seen, ideally, as exclusive and permanent, while acknowledging the existence of other patterns.

iv. . . . it is demystified, so that pupils are aware of the ways in which sexuality is exploited by advertisers and merchandisers, or unscrupulous individuals, so as to undermine the Christian view of marriage, and so as to shape their own views surreptitiously in ways which may harm the stability of their future marriage.

In key stages 3 & 4 (secondary education) governors may wish to ask further questions of both RE & the other relevant curriculum areas.

i. Are pupils made aware of the legal problems involved in cohabitation, as opposed to formal marriage?

ii. Are the valid possibilities of chastity and celibacy taught alongside other lifestyles when sexual relationships are discussed?

iii. Are the Christian ideals of lifelong, loyal marriage presented to the pupils, with arguments based not just on utilitarian expediency, or personal integrity, but on the nature of public commitment, and divine intention? Are teachers aware of subliminal signals which may subvert this – for instance, does the girl in the sex education film wear a ring? If not, the film is not morally neutral as its producers may claim, but skewed against Christian morality. There is no neutral ground, and pupils should be helped to see that sexuality is not amoral.

iv. Are pupils made aware or the dangers of placing too great a value on sexual success or satisfaction as an idol or source of personal salvation, so that this aspect of their lives is seen in perspective?

(b) Admissions etc.

It is hard to see an admissions policy (for which governors are also responsible in church-aided schools) being acceptable which discriminated against the children of cohabiting parents – but governors should be aware of the knock-on effect of other practices elsewhere. To give an extreme example, they may give children of regular communicants, or baptized children, prior claim on places at the school, which could affect children from a parish where cohabitants were refused communion, or cohabitants refused baptism for their children.

The details of why staff are selected are not likely to be public knowledge, but if governors were to rule out a candidate on the grounds that he was known to be cohabiting, they would need to be certain that their declared equal opportunities policy, and the terms of the advertisement, allowed for choices based on moral views as well as professional abilities.

In the event of ballots among parents where a contentious issue is bitterly contested, in connection with grant maintained status for instance, governors would do well to obtain specialist advice about which cohabiting, separated or divorced parents are eligible to vote.

2. The church

(a) Funerals

While the formal next of kin may well have the task of arranging the funeral, there may be a partner in the background who has no legal place, but is deeply involved emotionally in what goes on. The family may not have approved of the friendship, whether it was merely one of companionship or of sexual partnership. In other cases they may gladly involve the partner in arrangements. I suggest that a clergyman taking the funeral and meeting the bereaved where such a relationship is possible, should . . .

i.   . . . be aware of the possibility of a hidden partner and give attention to him or her in the service and in private comfort;

ii.   . . . choose a word to describe the relationship which is appropriate, not causing offence by saying either too much or too little about it;

iii. . . . give credit where credit is due for what was good in the relationship, and in the rest of the person's life, but . . .

iv . . . do not be false to his or her memory, or to Christian truth, in the way his life is acknowledged. The mourners will know a rough diamond, even if the preacher doesn't, and may actually value permission from him to own the ill as well as the good they think of the dead.

Perhaps these points are valid for any funeral, but this situation is particularly sensitive. At many funerals there will be other mourners who are cohabitant. How will those who are not technically 'in laws' be acknowledged when this is appropriate? They may have done the final nursing.

(b) Baptisms

Baptism policies are a bone of contention in many parishes, and can vary from unquestioning acceptance of all-comers, from within and outside the parish, to a rigid insistence on active church membership before a child is baptised. Within their own policy, in connection with cohabitation, clergy and PCCs might ask themselves whether:

i. . . . they wish to apply a different policy to children whose parents are cohabiting from that applied to children of single mothers alone or of married couples, and if so, what are their grounds;

ii. . . . they will accept god-parents who are cohabitants;

iii. . . . they would wish to make conditions about the marriage of the parents before arranging to baptize their child, not least because of the public promise to 'repent of my sins' given by parents and god-parents;

iv. . . . they want to include elements in the baptism service which will make clear the Christian ideals of conduct with regard to marriage and other matters.

For my own part, I adopt the same practice with all who ask for a child's baptism within the parish, asking that they and the godparents meet with me as I try to explain both what will happen in the service, and the Gospel message that is contained within it. I ask about the couple's intentions to do with marriage, but do not insist on it before the baptism. I do, however, point out some of the disadvantages for the child if its parents are not married. Knowing that many of the guests at baptisms are cohabiting, and in any case have probably not heard much of the lifestyle that Christians offer them, we have recently begun using the Ten Commandments in modern language in baptism services, rather than the simple summary. From time to time I would refer to the commitment and security of marriage in a baptism sermon, perhaps by way of illustration. Other clergy may feel this is a rather soft approach, and wish to be more direct; some may feel that even this is too pointed.

Baptism is not, of course, simply a rite for children, and cohabitants may be converted and wish to be baptized, or may be faced with their own need for commitment when they ask to have children baptized. I heard of one cohabiting couple who were baptized by immersion in their Anglican church and changed out of baptism robes straight into their wedding dress and suit for their marriage service to continue. I heard of another girl who sought baptism, and would have gladly married her cohabitant partner, but he was not willing. The questions that a PCC or cleric might ask in these circumstances will be about the intentions and commitment of the baptism candidate to the partnership or forthcoming marriage, and also whether they wish to apply more stringent rules to cohabitants than they do to baptism candidates who are involved, perhaps, in dubious business or have not spoken to their parents for a year. Hippolytus' teaching on marriage was referred to earlier in this book. It was part of a check-list of who might be admitted to baptism which did not isolate issues about marriage from issues about work and other aspects of living.

(c) Other sacraments and leadership

I referred above to the possibility that cohabitants might be refused communion. A church wishing to take this measure should ask itself whether this is the example of notorious evil living that it most wished to penalize, and if so it would presumably be a matter to discuss with the bishop. If an individual case involved blatant adultery, then I would be prepared to take that step. If that is not so, then the questions to ask are about the stability of the relationship. Is it stable, or moving towards marriage? Is the taking of communion together a sign that the couple want to intensify and ratify their relationship? Is it part of their exploration of God's guidance for them for their future? How best can the church help in that exploration? Will insistence on marriage or excommunication push the couple apart, or away from the church anyway, or together too hastily?

And what about a person who offers for some public role in the church? For an able teacher for a run-down Sunday school, or a trained counsellor, or keen committee member willing to rejuvenate a tired PCC, or a fluent reader anxious to go on the rota for lesson-reading, is cohabitation a bar to such office? Does the extra measure of public approval, and the implication that they represent an example for others, alter the situation for such people, as opposed to those who are simply taking communion with the crowd? I think it does, though that may seem inconsistent, and – for the record – have discouraged a nomination for the PCC on those grounds.

(d) Teaching and general church life

A parish might ask itself what opportunities it takes or makes to speak positively about marriage, and about singleness, in its weekly services, study and fellowship groups, youth work and in special meetings or events.

What opportunities can be made for this, perhaps using 'secular' festivals like (St) Valentine's day or days in the regular church cycle like the fourteenth Sunday after Pentecost, where talk of love is appropriate? What ways can be used to make our good news in this area of life known outside the circle of the church? Articles might be offered to local free papers or targeted invitations sent to those who have been or are going to be married in the church or even to cohabitants who show they are considering it.

What opportunity is given for parents of cohabitants, or others who are affected or anxious about the practice, to meet and share their concerns in prayer and mutual support?[1]

(e) Marriage

The circumstances in which a marriage in the Church of England can be refused if one of the parties lives within the parish are limited. Nevertheless, some clergy attempt to discourage a cohabiting couple from being married in their parish church. Others turn a blind eye to the couple's circumstances, though unless they have lied in completing the application form the fact that they live together can hardly be missed. In deciding how to act, these considerations are relevant:

i. If the church wishes not to marry those who have been cohabiting, how will the couple, and the wider community, interpret that policy? What steps will be taken to explain simply to the couple why their request is turned down?[2] Are there ways of conveying this explanation to the rest of their family? Will it be necessary to explain the policy publicly, either because a particular case hits the headlines, or as a means of teaching and forewarning the parish? If so, is the press release ready in advance, phrased so as to give a positive message?

ii. If the church is prepared to marry eligible cohabiting couples, how will the couple and the wider community interpret that policy? In what way does its normal preparation for marriage need to be adapted to meet their different circumstances? How can the church's teaching on marriage be affirmed in the community and among the couple's family and peers when it seems to condone a lesser form of relationship? In particular, two areas need to be addressed; how can the couple be helped through the changes that will occur in their relationship even if they do not expect them because of the marriage, and how can they be helped to grasp the seriousness of the vows they make of permanent and loyal love when their understanding may hitherto have been shaped by a degree of uncertainty?

To this end, will the church suggest, or require any change in the couple's circumstances prior to the marriage? For instance, should they be asked to live apart again until the wedding? (Difficult if they have a child.) Or should they be asked to bring forward the date to the earliest possible? (Awkward if the family are saving up for a big party in a year's time, or they cannot get a room for the reception.) What practical help is the church prepared to offer if there are such difficulties?[3]

iii. In conducting the marriage of former cohabitants, what adaptation might the church insist on, or offer, in the service? Is there to be some declaration of repentance, before or during the service? Will the minister declare that there ought to be repentance, even if the couple are unwilling? Will the sermon or the prayers reflect the situation without labouring the point? Might an appropriate hymn serve this purpose? Is some alteration in the ritual, such as the couple entering the church together and the absence of any 'giving away' of the bride, as appropriate as words as a way of being true to the couple, to the church's teaching, and to their circumstances?

My own practice comes within the ambit of sections ii and iii above. In the service itself I use extra prayers (see the appendix) and something appropriate to the couple in the sermon. On one occasion a couple used the hymn, *Dear Lord and Father of mankind, forgive our foolish ways,* to open their service. On the few occasions I have mentioned it, no one has taken up the possibility of not being given away. Perhaps it was dad, not the bride, who felt cheated over that.

In the preparation of any couple I use phrases from the various prayer books to highlight the exclusive nature of marriage, and marriage as the right place to enjoy sexual relations with security and confidence, while we are discussing which service to use. I also stress the key importance to Christian and English legal understandings of marriage of consent and commitment, as enshrined in the words 'I will.' How much of this is taken in is, of course, difficult to gauge, especially if the couple have their own agenda, like wondering whether they can bring in flowers, and do we have a red carpet or a choir? Such questions are on my agenda too, but lower down the list. Thus in these areas what I say with cohabitants is not markedly different from what I say with others. I say less about sexual compatibility, and possible problems of that nature, but do make a point of asking how they think their relationship will change once they are married. If they reply that they do not think it will, as most do, it is a matter of suggesting areas where others have found change – areas of possible danger, as well as greater security, such as a feeling of being trapped or caught, or a tendency not to try so hard to be pleasing, since the legal ties are stronger and courtship has to do less work.

As a final note, there are claims that the Church of England would be better able to affirm the value of Christian marriage if it were not bound legally to celebrate the marriage of all comers. This issue is ably discussed in *An Honourable Estate* published at the behest of the General Synod in 1988. Those arguments are not particularly affected by the issue of cohabitation. If we were relieved of an obligation to marry, it would enable those who wished it to pursue a rigorist line in refusing blatant or unrepentant cohabitants. I suspect, however, that this form of disestablishment would enable the refused couple to move more freely to a church where the service would be taken without any need for qualifications of parochial residence or regular worship.

Notes

1. This particular example is given by Ted Pratt on p. 21 of his booklet *Living in Sin?* While I do not take Pratt's line, I recognize that it can be useful in provoking thought as a policy is worked out. Correspondence with him has helped to tighten up my own ideas.
2. One might add, more polemically, how can you explain acceptably that their request for what they see as Christian

marriage has been turned down by the organization which is supposed to dispense Christian marriages? Are they not trying to regularize their relationship and so opt into what the church teaches is the only proper sexual relationship? There is a valid answer, but it may need to be in a thirty second sound bite.

3. Again a point made by Pratt, in connection with the encouragement of couples to marry even if they cannot afford the reception, rather than cohabit until they can. Other clergy whom I know have offered discounts for a limited period – to encourage cohabitants so splice the knot, or package deals with the church hall, caterers and florist, to achieve a less expensive 'do'.

APPENDIX I

Discussion material and magazine articles*

'Common Law' marriage: some cases and questions to discuss

These were written originally for a clergy conference, but could be adapted to fit a discussion group, class, or other local meeting.

1. You meet a man who has often called at your vicarage asking for cups of tea, food, baksheesh, etc., and he joyfully tells you that he now has a flat, with his girlfriend and their baby. He speaks (genuinely) about his wasted years, and his hopes for the future. He shows you his wages slip to prove that he is now making good, and assures you that he and his girlfriend do intend to marry. What are your reactions? (Bear in mind that the local authority does not have flats to allocate to single homeless men, but gives high points to mothers with children and that an address is necessary both for DSS payments and on most job applications.) Where, if anywhere, is the sin in this situation?

2. Your second cousin's daughter has left her husband, taking with her their two children. He had treated her badly, physically and mentally, and she was both depressed and

* The author intends items in this appendix, and prayers in the next, for readers' use, and they may be reproduced and adapted freely for non-commercial use, provided their source is acknowledged. The typesetting remains Copyright © HarperCollins*Publishers* 1994, and permission to photocopy should be sought from them.

demoralized. She has now taken up with a single man, who was himself lacking in confidence, and they are living together and have been for over a year, and are gradually rebuilding each other's lives and finding stability and security. Your cousin is uncertain how to react as a Christian to this situation. What advice would you give?

3. As vicar of Longtown on Solway you are asked to induct into the local Mothers' Union a lady who has begun attending the church with her family and is joining in quite keenly with its activities, even though that means crossing the five or so miles from the other side of the river Sark. It is to be a separate service, and in chatting about it with her you suggest that her husband might like to come as well. She hesitates, and looks a little uncertain, saying that they have not actually been married. How do you react, and do you break the news to the MU (bearing in mind that the village on the other side of the Sark is called Gretna and she is a resident in Scotland)?

4. A neighbour asks to chat with you to clarify his thoughts. He has been living with his girlfriend for over a year, but is uncertain about his next step. He felt hurt and let down several times by other women, and his parents had a very stormy relationship. He finds in his present girlfriend a great deal of support, and has been able to help her, he reckons, over the trauma of having to leave her former partner and cope with their children alone and fearful of the partner's threats to her. Neither he nor she feels confident in themselves that they can live up to the ideals of married commitment. Your advice? Or perhaps your method of enabling his decision?

5. John and Jane lived in Berwick-upon-Tweed. Both held down good jobs, and neither contributed more than the other to their household, except that it was John who bought the house with a legacy to himself shortly before

they met. They had no children, and felt that legal marriage would somehow demean their relationship, though they were known as husband and wife locally and never told people otherwise. John always put off making a will, and following his sudden death Jane finds that his next of kin is a brother in London, with whom he never got on, but who still expects to inherit the bulk of his estate. Discuss where justice lies in this situation. (As a non-dependent Jane cannot claim support under the provisions of the Inheritance (Provision for Dependents) Act. One mile further north and she could have sought a retrospective marriage by declarator.)

6. A couple approach you about the baptism of their child. They have been living together for a while, and have bought the house jointly, registered the child jointly in the father's name, and throw out in conversation that they ought to see you about a wedding. They are friendly enough to you, and eventually you get the banns form back, but they twice defer the wedding, once explicitly on financial grounds. How would you handle this?

A 'flier' reprinted from a parish magazine

This has been used, with adaptation, in a local free-paper, and as part of a package given to couples asking for their child's baptism.

If you really care

I recently led a discussion among clergy about the increasingly common practice of living together before or instead of formal marriage. Here are some things a couple in that situation should do to provide for each other and their children as effectively as if they had married – if they care enough to do so. It is tongue in cheek, perhaps, but no joke.

1. Draw up an agreement about who owns your bank accounts (even the housekeeping). (See a lawyer?)
2. Vet your house conveyance; who has beneficial interest? (See a lawyer.)
3. Make mutually beneficial wills (See a lawyer).
4. Fill in the forms to acknowledge paternity of your children.
5. The woman should specify the father by name as his children's guardian in her will (see a lawyer). He cannot adopt them until her death, but if he then does they are legitimized.
6. Make sure you have insurances which allow you to nominate each other as beneficiaries. Ditto company or personal pension.
7. Etc. etc!
   (Note that for those who avoid marriage so as to keep the law out to their bedrooms, this is not an easy option.)
8. Commit matrimony (and reregister children?).
9. Alternatively, emigrate to Scotland (and see a lawyer).

Another magazine article

Happy ever after?

Perhaps twenty-five couples a year get married in St Wilfrid's Church, and in the service we refer to them being joined in 'Christian Marriage'. I sometimes wonder whether that gives the right impression.

I don't mean that there is anything wrong with what the couples are doing or what they intend, but is it the service in church in itself which makes 'Christian marriage'? In fact it has only been the last few hundred years that either the church or the law has *required* the presence of the vicar, or a ceremony in church, even though for centuries this has probably been normal practice. Have we been hoodwinked by the outward trappings of 'the day'?

In some ways we have, so that some couples put off their wedding, even though they live together and have a family, until they can afford it – it being an elaborate ceremony in full dress with a splendid reception afterwards. I believe it is right to celebrate a wedding, though I do think sometimes the festivities can go over the top. It gives the couple the chance to declare publicly their relationship, and celebrate each other's value while thanking parents, friends, other relatives and everyone who has contributed to their lives as they have grown up. The 'rite of passage' is worth it for that alone, whatever you think of the green certificate – but is that Christian marriage? Not in itself.

To have sufficient pride in one's spouse to make the relationship public (even before a few witnesses only) and to seek God's blessing for it, have been two of the hallmarks of Christian marriage, but only two. From the Bible it is possible to draw up a list of them, and these are expressed in one way or another in our wedding services. It is possible to measure both the present legal framework for marriage in this country, and any individual relationship (and that conceivably includes some 'common-law marriages') to see how they square up.

A clear intention in the Bible is that marriage should be a permanent relationship (even if it all too often fails to be because of hardheartedness – (Mark, 10:5-9). The lack of such an intention for permanence faults many 'common law' relationships, though not all – but it also faults the law itself. (Incidentally, though the phrase 'common law marriage' is convenient it carries no legal weight at all south of the Scottish border.)

Marriage is clearly intended to be a sexually exclusive relationship – no one else should get a look in. 'Thou shalt not commit adultery'. But such exclusive loyalty (or at least a sense of hurt and outrage when loyalty is broken) is also to be found among cohabitees. I have met a number of moralists who talk as if cohabitation meant the same as promiscuity. This misrepresents many people who are after their own lights very faithful.

Companionship and support are highlighted in our marriage services, in a way which emphasizes a deeper meaning to 'love' than is sometimes understood. Romantic and erotic love have their obvious place in Christian marriage (though the romantic bit has not always had as high a profile as it does now). However, it is the commitment to care and support lovingly in 'worse' as well as 'better' that is specially Christian about love, just as God loves us even when we do not respond to that love.

A friend who has spent some time in India highlighted a feature of marriage which we in England often overlook despite a new phrase in Section 6 of the 1980 service – that it involves a commitment to care for the wider family. Are those attempting 'trial marriage' – logically impossible – really looking over their mothers-in-law, on approval?

For many reasons I would push marriage, but I stress that the commitment to each other's good in Christian marriage is more than getting it right legally.

APPENDIX II

Prayers for Marriage

The options open to Church of England clerics taking a marriage service are limited. For reasons of English law, as much as ecclesiastical discipline, they must use one of the prescribed services – from the Book of Common Prayer, the Alternative Service Book, or with the bishop's authority, the 1928/1966 rite. We are not free to alter those words, though additions by way of sermons, readings and addresses, and extra prayers are in order. Members of non-established churches are required to include the forms prescribed by Section 44(3) of the 1949 Marriage Act, but beyond that may follow the practice – rigid or liberal – of their denomination.

Preparing for the service

We are all faced with a variety of expectations from couples preparing for their wedding day. Some will come with no ideas at all, 'We'll leave it to you,' they say, when asked about hymns or music. Others choose those items, perhaps remembering them from schooldays, or prompted by Gran, and have service sheets printed, without consultation, and blithely expect to sing

> '. . . forgive our foolish ways,
>   reclothe us in our rightful minds. . .'

immediately after making the most profound promises of their lives, for which an unsound mind would be grounds for annulment. Few, at least in my Anglican experience, come prepared in the way some highly articulate Unitarian friends of mine came, ready to speak to each other during the service and in front of their friends about the qualities they appreciated most in each other. The most that I am used to is a request for a particular reading, or for a poem to be read, or some original ideas for the music, or for a friend or dear member of their family to be remembered in a prayer.

While I have reservations about that last request, especially at the festivities of a wedding, I believe we should encourage couples to make the service their own in this sort of way, and where possible help them to achieve it. That is none too easy in my experience. Some couples expect the vicar to choose the hymns and everything else for them. Like most clergy, I suppose, I have a list of possible hymns which I give to the couples along with an information sheet about costs and other details. I sometimes have to sing bits of them before they are recognized. They take away copies of the service, which include the selection of prayers and readings, and some will specify which of these they want. They may also see the organist, and choose music with him. Failure to do this can lead to complications if they request, for instance, 'Ave Maria' of which there are several versions by different composers, or 'The Trumpet Voluntary', which conveys different pieces to different people. There is a delightful story, whose truth I cannot vouch for, of a bride who asked as her entry piece for the theme song of the film 'Robin Hood, Prince of Thieves', a recent successful pop single, with some words not inappropriate to a wedding. The organist took this to be the 1960s TV jingle, and played 'Robin Hood, Robin Hood, riding through the glen' with great gusto. On a more sublime note, at a recent wedding here in Northenden a drama teacher arranged for a colleague to read one of Shakespeare's love sonnets. For her that was right, for others the pop song, perhaps on tape rather than attempted by a classically trained organist, is more fitting – so long as its words are not a lament after desertion. I suggest a possible text for remembrance later.

Using the marriage service

The set Anglican services for marriage itself offer no variation to take into account a couple's circumstances, other than omission of the prayer about childbearing (section 26), and a limited selection of prayers (section 31ff.) with permission to use others or to extemporize. There is, however, a service of prayer and dedication available for use after a civil marriage.[1] This is not explicitly stated to be for use with those who have been divorced, but the tone of the rubrics and optional confession imply it.

When a couple's circumstances include either a past divorce or cohabitation, I feel that the lack of variation available is a fault. It is as if their own past and their integrity are being denied by a liturgy written with what seems to be starry-eyed naïveté on the part of the church. The ASB introduction (section 6), for instance, lacks even the mild insistence of '1928' that marriage is 'an honourable estate'. That introduction is probably the only occasion when most people (whether cohabitant or not) hear any Christian teaching on marriage. It teaches not only the couple, but their friends and families, what we intend and expect as a result of the ceremony. Just as Cranmer in his Introduction had to affirm the value of marriage over and against the twin errors of casual fornication and the mediaeval idolization of monastic celibacy, so we in this generation need to affirm its value as an outward and public sign of commitment, and of the couple's pride in each other.

But not all churches in the Anglican Communion are as slow as we are. The recent report of the Kanamai Consultation of African Anglicans *African Culture and African Liturgy* suggests, in the section devoted to marriage, not only a distinct service for the blessing of a civil marriage, but also separate provision for the remarriage of divorcées, and also for the blessing of 'customary marriages', i.e., the marriages of those who were married in traditional ways other than a Christian ceremony or a secular state registration. It is to such 'customary' marriage that committed cohabitation or 'Common Law' marriage in Britain seems to me to approximate, and I believe that we can learn from our African colleagues. They ask the question: 'Is customary marriage complete in itself or does it necessarily require the sanctioning of the church?'; but they also suggest that the marriage liturgy should provide for thanksgiving for couples who have lived together in love, albeit in customary marriage.[2] They also suggest a distinctive service for use after civil weddings.

Some British pastors have attempted to bring home the weaknesses of simple cohabitation by writing additional prefaces to supplement the official introductions when a couple have been cohabiting prior to their wedding day.[3] There are two dangers here, I believe. One is that the prefaces that I have seen tend to be rather condemnatory, singling out that couple. The other is that it is all present at all marriages who need to be reminded of the Christian ideal of love, security and truth offered to them for their adoption in the words of the introduction. (As the rarely used homily in the marriage service of the Book of Common Prayer indicates in its opening sentence.) I therefore believe that the introduction for all marriages should be expanded to include these points. Liturgists may improve my wording, but I suggest that when revision is carried out, something such as this be added as a third paragraph in the ASB order (section 6):

> It is God's purpose that man and woman declare publicly their love and the pride they have in each other, and that their community recognize and support them in their commitment; it is his purpose that such avowed commitment be a defence for them against temptations to fall short of the ideal of loyalty and love which he sets before us in Christ.

While I believe that the introduction is the place for general teaching about marriage, it is in the prayers that variation may make the service appropriate to the couple's own circumstances. Unless they specifically ask for it – and perhaps not even then – the public service is not the place for a confession.

Privately perhaps it may be right, either as formal prayer or as a recognition in discussion with the minister and in fact before God, that all has not been right in their past. Cohabitation is not the only thing that might be recognized in such a discussion, and I would hesitate to press the point. It does neither the church nor the couple any good to make some sort of confession a hoop for them to jump through before they can get a church wedding. Nor should cohabitation or divorce be the only practices for which the church *demands* public confession of an explicit nature.

However, the integrity both of the church and the couple is at stake in the service. This is true not only when they have been living together for perhaps some years, but also if there has been a divorce, or previous deep relationships. It is no credit to them if the only words we can offer them assume that they are coming without any previous relationship from their parents' homes. And such prayers give the church the appearance of a naïve detachment from the real world. But while most of the couple's peers will know of their history, there may be others present at the wedding who do not know or want to know such details – grandparents, perhaps. Their sensitivities should not be trespassed upon by going into too much elaboration. Like a juggler with many clubs in the air the minister at a wedding has many individuals' circumstances to consider. The prayers which I suggest below do therefore have an element of ambiguity, to allow each participant and each guest to clothe them with their own knowledge of the couple.

Almighty Father,
who alone know all the forces which mould or mar
    our life and our loves:
forgive us for what has been wrong in our pasts;
heal the hurts which scar our memories;
help us to correct the failings in our present lives,
    and direct and enrich our future:
    through Jesus Christ our Saviour.   Amen

(Originally written in connection with the remarriage of divorcés, this may be appropriate for many weddings, since like the old shoes and tin cans that used to be tied behind wedding cars, we all carry some unhelpful baggage with us to our marriages, whether we know it or not.)

Loving Lord,
whose eternal love is reflected in all that is rich and good
 in human love,
we thank you for the journey of love
 which N & n have travelled together;
we thank you that in love they have come to this
 commitment of marriage,
and pray that they may continue forward together
 all their life long in the light of your love;
through your redeeming power.   Amen.

(This was written with cohabitation in mind. It does not emphasize the details of the couple's past, but allows them, their peers, their families and the church to be honest about it. A wedding is one step along the journey of life – a step some take further along the journey than others.)

Almighty God,
who hate nothing that you have made,
and forgive the errors of those who put their trust in you;
in our love for each other we have taken hastily
 steps which are right in their own time;
in our thought for each other we have hurt
 those whose thoughts were for us;
in your mercy forgive us where we have erred,
help us to forgive those who have hurt us,
and so take the imperfections of our lives
that they are transformed to reflect your love;
through Jesus Christ our redeemer.   Amen

(This was written in an attempt to give words to those who may wish to express repentance for the way they have approached their relationship. No one set of words can cater for all that people have been through and may wish to say; these need to be fleshed out in prior discussion if not in the prayer itself. It was intended for private use, rather than as part of the public service.[4]

God our Father,
you show us your love as we share in your creation
    through the gift and care of children.
Bless N & n, as they care for their children
    now and in the future;
help them to be patient and understanding,
    wise and even-handed,
    so that their children may be sure of their love
    and may grow up happy and responsible,
    to know and love you in your Son Jesus Christ.   Amen.

(This prayer, based on ASB prayers from the Thanksgiving and Marriage services, is intended for use when a couple already have children of their own together, or from previous marriages. It might be suitable at section 25 of the ASB Marriage service, if the lawyers will allow it. The ASB authors apparently chose the word 'gift' in section 26 to allow for adoption, but that is a very subtle allowance.)

Father of all, we recognize with gratitude
    the many ways in which other people –
    our families and friends – contribute to our lives;
we thank you for those, present today or absent,
who have helped N. and n. on their way, especially . . . .
and we pray that, living up to the good examples before them
N. and n. may be in their turn a source of blessing to others;
    Through Jesus Christ our Lord.   Amen.

(This is written in an attempt to meet, in a manner fitting for a wedding celebration, the request to pray 'for' a deceased relative or friend. Quite apart from the issues to do with prayers *for* the dead, it seems to me that a prayer focusing on someone else, probably unknown to at least half of those present, interrupts the flow of the marriage liturgy. This prayer attempts to integrate the past with the event of the day and its hopes.)

Praying and preaching about marriage at other services

The wedding service is not the only time when marriage should be mentioned in Christian worship and teaching. The ASB lectionary highlights 'the family' on Pentecost 14. I recently used the excuse that St Valentine's day fell on a Sunday to invite as many couples as I could trace who had been married in this parish to a special 'reunion' (was that the right word I wonder) service. But even that can have pitfalls. At the door afterwards I was upbraided by one – single – lady, who asked if I realized how many people in the congregation were, like her through no fault of their own but through the circumstances perhaps of war, single or widowed. I was rather put out, since it was that very thought that had deterred me from taking up the subject for a dozen years. If I had dealt with the issue more often, perhaps she would not have been so upset.

We need to grasp the nettle, both of teaching about marriage, and about singleness, and how both can be the calling of God. We do that not just in a sermon, but in hymns and prayers – but those prayers, I believe, need to be robust enough to wrestle with the problems of married life, of loneliness, of tentative and half-trusting relationships, and those who are hurt by failures as well as blessed by success. It is a fine sentiment, but somewhat sentimental, merely to pray 'bless all who are married and every parent and child,' without wrestling before God as to what that blessing might mean. After all, even the advertisers are now recognizing that the ideal family of consumers may well be split.

I speak of wrestling before God, because I am aware that in some issues at least there are no easy answers or that there will be some people who will be disquieted by the answers others come up with and try to live out. Most of all I should not wish to pray,'Dear God, you've just heard my sermon; now deliver the goods'. I exaggerate, though the sermon, if it is worthwhile, will have set the people of God thinking what the ideal might be that he sets before us to work towards. In such circumstances a litany, coming to the problem from the different standpoints involved, may be a more helpful form of prayer than a collect or *ex tempore* monologue.[5] What follows was used, alongside the more conventional 'Mothers' Union Prayer' at a service in which we were bringing to God the issue of cohabitation. It used between each section the verse and response:

Lord in your mercy, *Hear our prayer*

For those who live together in commitment before marriage; that it may be a worthy preparation and that their relationship may grow deeper and firmer with their public commitment, . . .

For those considering the commitment of marriage, but whose circumstances or experience make that commitment difficult to make; that growing trust of themselves and knowledge of their partner will enable them to make the right decision, . . .

For those who live apart during their engagement; that God will honour their restraint and that their love and understanding may grow stronger as they come to marriage, . . .

For those whose relationship is casual, ill-conceived or self-centred; that they may learn greater understanding of themselves, and greater responsibility towards each other . . .

For those in the media, the law, the church and in society at large who shape attitudes to marriage and human relationships; that their influence may be wholesome and shaped by God, . . .

For those who are hurt by current attitudes to marriage, whether they are scandalized as onlookers, or affected as victims of man's inhumanity to woman, and woman's to man, . . .

For us all; that we may hold a right balance between the

law of God which is graciously given for our guidance and correction, and the forgiveness of God who in his grace renews our lives and enables us to live and work towards a wholesome future, . . .

For us all; that in all our family relationships we may conscientiously seek the will of God and live it out towards our parents, children and peers with the grace and truth that are in Christ, . . .

I offer this not as *the* litany about cohabitation, but as a sample of what might be written and used, and invite – challenge – readers to improve upon it and perhaps adapt its clauses to the need of individuals they know. The Mothers' Union prayer mentioned above runs as follows:

Almighty God our heavenly Father,
who gave marriage to be a source of blessing to mankind,
we thank you for the joys of family life.
Pour out upon us your Holy Spirit,
that we may truly love and serve you.
Bless all who are married, and every parent and child.
May we know your peace and presence in our homes;
fill them with your love and use them for your glory.
Bless the members of the Mothers' Union throughout the
   world;
unite us in prayer and worship, love and service,
that strengthened by your grace
we may seek to do your will;
   through Jesus Christ our Lord.   Amen.
                    Reproduced by permission
                    of the Mothers' Union

Notes

1. *Services of Prayer and Dedication after Civil Marriage.* CIO London 1985. These services are 'commended by the House of Bishops'.

2. *African Culture and African Liturgy: the report of the Kanamai Consultation on this theme (31st May-4th June 1993), with an introduction by Bishop David Gitari.* Grove, Nottingham 1993, quotations from p. 14. As far as I know, the associated liturgical texts have not yet been published (December 1993).

3. E.g. as cited by Edward Pratt, *Living in Sin?* St Simon's Church, Portsmouth, 1991, pp.25, 26.

4. These prayers, with slight variations, were first published in my *Marriage before Marriage?* Grove Nottingham 1988 pp.14f. cf. p.10f. the first having been broadcast on teletext at the time of General Synod's debate on remarriage of divorcées.

5. I owe the idea of a litany as the means to pray through a difficult moral issue to Prof. O.M.T. O'Donovan, in his Grove anniversary lecture. *Liturgy and Ethics*, Nottingham 1993 p. 10f.